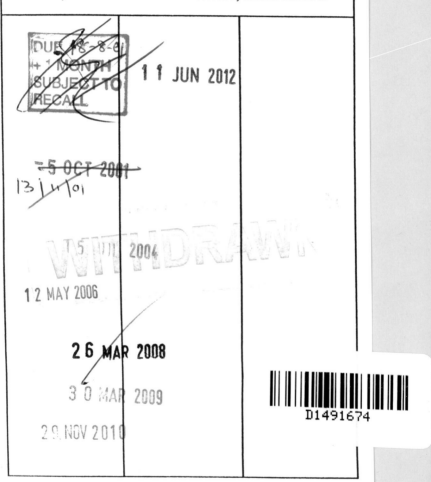

A MEDITATION
HANDBOOK

Also by Geshe Kelsang Gyatso

Meaningful to Behold
Clear Light of Bliss
Buddhism in the Tibetan Tradition
Heart of Wisdom
Joyful Path of Good Fortune
Universal Compassion
Guide to Dakini Land

Contents

Illustrations

Acknowledgements

This text, *A Meditation Handbook*, is an important practical Buddhist meditation manual. It was written by Venerable Geshe Kelsang Gyatso during a meditation retreat at Tharpaland in Scotland. Our heartfelt gratitude goes out to the author for his great kindness in providing such clear guidelines to the spiritual path, and for presenting a straightforward way of integrating the vital practice of meditation into our daily lives.

The main responsibility for editing the text and endnotes was undertaken by Michael Garside and we thank him for his excellent work, all carried through with great dedication.

Our thanks also go to Gelong Thubten Gyatso for his valuable assistance in improving the final manuscript, and to Hugh Clift, Mariana Libano, Gordon Ellis, and Thomas, Inge and Stephen Garside for their many helpful suggestions.

We would also like to express our appreciation for the kind assistance of Geoff Jukes, who provided generous financial support to the editor to ensure that the work could go ahead.

May this priceless handbook bring the fruit of pure happiness to many beings.

Roy Tyson, Director
Manjushri Institute
November 1989

Editorial Note

Since this book is a manual for meditation practice, the explanations of the various Lamrim topics have been kept very simple and concise. Those who wish to study Lamrim in more detail should study *Joyful Path of Good Fortune* by Geshe Kelsang Gyatso, which is an extensive commentary to the Stages of the Path.

Preface

The twenty-one meditation practices presented in this book are the essential practices of the Stages of the Path, or Lamrim in Tibetan. Lamrim is a special set of instructions that includes all the essential teachings of Buddha Shakyamuni, arranged in such a way that all his Hinayana and Mahayana[1] teachings can be put into practice in a single meditation session. It was compiled by the great Indian Buddhist Master Atisha, who was invited to Tibet by King Jang Chub Ö in AD 1042 and spent the rest of his life there spreading pure Dharma.[2] There is a completely pure and unbroken lineage of these Lamrim instructions from Buddha Shakyamuni down to our present-day Spiritual Guides.

Many great Kadampa teachers have said that it is far more important to gain experience of Lamrim than it is to achieve clairvoyance, miracle powers or high social status. This is true because in previous lives we have often possessed clairvoyance and potent miracle powers, and many times in the past we have been in the highest positions in the human and god realms. Despite this, we continue to experience uncontrolled rebirth and physical and mental suffering caused by anger, attachment, jealousy and confusion. If we gain deep experience of Lamrim there will be no basis for these problems; we will be completely free from all of them.

First we must understand the value of Lamrim. Then, by joyfully and patiently doing these meditations, we will gradually experience the fruits of Lamrim practice. Eventually we will attain the freedom from all suffering and the unchanging peace and happiness of full enlightenment.

Geshe Kelsang Gyatso
Tharpaland
November 1989

PART ONE

Foundations and Preliminaries

Buddha Shakyamuni

Introduction

WHAT IS MEDITATION?

Meditation is a method for acquainting our mind with virtue. The more familiar our mind is with virtue, the calmer and more peaceful it becomes. When our mind is peaceful we are free from worries and mental discomfort and we experience true happiness. If our mind is not peaceful, then even if we have the most pleasant external conditions we will not be happy. However, if we train our mind to become peaceful we will be happy all the time, even in the most adverse conditions. Therefore it is important to train our mind through meditation.

There are two types of meditation: analytical meditation and placement meditation. When we contemplate the meaning of a Dharma instruction that we have heard or read we are doing analytical meditation. By deeply contemplating the instruction, eventually we reach a conclusion or cause a specific virtuous state of mind to arise. This is the object of placement meditation. Having found our object through analytical meditation, we then concentrate on it single-pointedly for as long as possible in order to become deeply acquainted with it. This single-pointed concentration is placement meditation. Usually, the term 'meditation' is used to refer to placement meditation, while analytical meditation is often referred to simply as 'contemplation'. Placement meditation depends upon contemplation and contemplation depends upon listening to or reading Dharma teachings.

THE OBJECTS OF MEDITATION

In general, any wholesome object can be used as an object of meditation. If we discover that by acquainting our mind with a particular object our mind becomes more peaceful and wholesome, this indicates that for us the object is wholesome. If the opposite happens, this shows that for us it is an unwholesome object. Many objects are neutral and have no particular positive or negative effect on our mind.

There are many wholesome objects of meditation, but the most meaningful are those explained in this book – the visualization of the assembly of Buddhas[3] and Bodhisattvas[4] as described on page 16, and the objects contained in the twenty-one meditation practices, from meditation on relying on a Spiritual Guide[5] to meditation on emptiness,[6] the ultimate nature of phenomena.

By relying on a qualified Spiritual Guide we open the door to practising Dharma. Through the blessings of our Spiritual Guide we generate faith and confidence in our practice and we easily attain all the realizations of the Stages of the Path. For these reasons we need to meditate on relying on a Spiritual Guide.

We need to meditate on this precious human life in order to realize that we now have a special opportunity to practise Dharma. If we appreciate the great potential of this life we will not waste it by engaging in meaningless activities. We need to meditate on death and impermanence in order to overcome procrastination and to ensure that our Dharma practice is pure by overcoming our preoccupation with worldly concerns. If we practise Dharma purely it is not so difficult to attain realizations. By meditating on the danger of lower rebirth, taking refuge sincerely, and avoiding non-virtue and practising virtue, we protect ourselves from taking lower rebirth and ensure that life after life we will obtain a precious human rebirth endowed with all the conditions conducive to the practice of Dharma.

We need to meditate on the sufferings of humans and gods so that we develop a spontaneous wish to achieve permanent liberation, or nirvana. This wish, known as 'renunciation', strongly encourages us to complete the practice of the spiritual paths, which are the actual methods to attain full liberation.

We need to meditate on love, compassion, and bodhichitta[7] so that we can overcome our self-cherishing and develop and maintain a good heart towards all living beings. With this good heart we need to meditate on tranquil abiding and superior seeing so that we can eradicate our ignorance and finally become a Buddha by abandoning the two types of obstruction.

Besides these, there are many other objects of meditation. For example, if we wish to meditate on the breath, we should do so in conjunction with the practices of taking and giving explained on pages 83 and 89. This meditation is very meaningful. If we devote too much time to ordinary breathing meditation, we may find we do not have enough time for our main practice, meditation on the Stages of the Path.

DEVELOPING THE WISH TO MEDITATE

If we examine our lives we will probably discover that most of our time and energy is directed towards mundane aims such as seeking material and emotional security, enjoying the pleasures of the senses, or achieving a good reputation. Although these things can make us happy for a short time, they are not able to provide the deep and lasting contentment we long for. Sooner or later our happiness turns into dissatisfaction and we find ourselves engaged in the pursuit of more worldly pleasures. Directly or indirectly, worldly pleasures cause us mental and physical suffering by stimulating attachment, jealousy, and frustration. Moreover, seeking to fulfil our own desires often brings us into conflict with others.

If true fulfilment cannot be found in worldly pleasures, where can it be found? Happiness is a state of mind, therefore the real source of happiness lies in the mind, not in external conditions. If our mind is pure and peaceful we will be happy, regardless of our external circumstances, but if it is impure and unpeaceful we will never find happiness, no matter how much we try to change our external conditions.

The purpose of Dharma practice is to cultivate those states of mind that are conducive to peace and well-being, and to eradicate those that are not. Only human beings can do this. Animals can enjoy food and sex, find homes, hoard wealth, subdue their enemies, and protect their family, but they cannot completely eliminate suffering and achieve lasting happiness. It would be a great shame if we were to use our precious human life only to achieve results that even animals can achieve. If we wish to avoid such a wasted life and fulfil the real purpose of being born human we must devote ourselves to the practice of the Stages of the Path.

THE PURPOSE OF MEDITATION

According to the Lamrim instructions, we can engage in a meditation practice with any one of three levels of motivation. The first level, the motivation of the initial scope, is to practise in order to protect ourselves from the danger of taking lower rebirth by ensuring that in future lives we achieve a precious human rebirth endowed with all the conditions necessary for the practice of Dharma. The second level, the motivation of the intermediate scope, is to practise in order to protect ourselves from any kind of uncontrolled rebirth by attaining liberation from cyclic existence. The third level, the motivation of the great scope, is to practise in order to achieve full enlightenment or Buddhahood so that we can benefit all living beings. These three levels of motivation are progressive. By engaging in meditation practices with the motivation of the initial scope we lay the foundation for advancing to the second level, and by engaging in meditation practices with the motivation of the intermediate scope we lay the foundation for advancing to the third level. All the essential practices of these three scopes are included within the twenty-one meditation practices presented in this book.

4

BACKGROUND KNOWLEDGE REQUIRED FOR
MEDITATION

Since the meditations presented in this book assume a belief in rebirth, or reincarnation, a brief description of the process of death and rebirth, and the places in which we can be reborn may be helpful.

The mind is neither physical nor a by-product of purely physical processes, but is a formless continuum that is a separate entity from the body. When the body disintegrates at death the mind does not cease. Although our superficial conscious mind ceases, it does so by dissolving into a deeper level of consciousness, the very subtle mind,[8] and the continuum of the very subtle mind has no beginning and no end. It is this mind which, when thoroughly purified, transforms into the omniscient mind of a Buddha.

Every action we perform leaves an imprint on our very subtle mind, and each imprint eventually gives rise to its own effect. Our mind is like a field and performing actions is like sowing seeds in that field. Virtuous actions sow seeds of future happiness and non-virtuous actions sow seeds of future suffering. The seeds we have sown in the past remain dormant until the conditions necessary for their germination come together. In some cases this can be many lifetimes after the original action was performed.

The seeds that ripen when we die are very important because they determine what kind of rebirth we will take. Which particular seed ripens at death depends upon the state of mind in which we die. If we die with a peaceful mind, this will stimulate a virtuous seed and we will experience a fortunate rebirth, but if we die with an unpeaceful mind, in a state of anger, say, this will stimulate a non-virtuous seed and we will experience an unfortunate rebirth. This is similar to the way in which nightmares are triggered by our being in an agitated state of mind just before falling asleep. The analogy is not accidental, for death closely resembles the process of falling asleep. In both cases the gross waking mind dissolves into the subtle mind and there follows a period of unconsciousness undisturbed by dreams. Later, due to movement of the energy winds[9] associated with the subtle mind, dreams occur. During sleep there is still a connection between the mind and the gross physical body, which is why dreams eventually end and we wake up, but after death this connection is completely severed.

For a period of up to forty-nine days after death the consciousness wanders in a dream-like state, known as the intermediate state, or bardo in Tibetan. At this time we experience different visions which arise from the karmic seeds[10] that were activated immediately before death. If negative seeds were activated the visions will be nightmarish, but if positive seeds were activated the visions will be predominantly pleasant. In either case, when the karmic seeds have matured sufficiently they impel the person to take rebirth in one of the six realms of cyclic existence.

The six realms are actual places in which we may be reborn. They are brought into existence through the power of our actions, and, since physical and verbal actions are initiated by mental intentions, ultimately the six realms are created by our mind. For example, a hell realm is a place that arises as a result of the worst actions, such as murder or extreme mental or physical cruelty, which depend upon the most deluded states of mind.

To form a mental image of the six realms we can compare them to the floors of a large, old house. In this analogy the house represents cyclic existence, or samsara in Sanskrit, the cycle of death and rebirth that ordinary beings must undergo without choice or control. This house has three storeys above ground, and three basements below. Deluded sentient beings are like the inhabitants of this house. They are continually moving up and down the house, sometimes living on the top floor, sometimes in the basement.

The ground floor corresponds to the human realm. Above this, on the first floor, is the realm of the demi-gods, non-human beings who are continually at war with the gods. In terms of power and prosperity they are superior to humans, but they are so obsessed with jealousy and violence that their lives have little spiritual value.

On the top floor live the gods. The lower classes of gods, the desire realm gods, live a life of ease and luxury, devoting their time to enjoyment and the satisfaction of their desires. Though their world is a paradise and their lifespan is very long, they are not immortal and they eventually fall to lower states. Since their lives are filled with distractions it is difficult for them to find the motivation to practise Dharma, so from a spiritual point of view a human life is more meaningful.

Higher than the desire realm gods are the gods of the form and formless realms. Having passed beyond sensual desire, the form realm gods experience the refined bliss of meditative absorption and possess bodies made of light. Transcending even these subtle forms, the gods of the formless realm abide without form in a subtle consciousness that resembles infinite space. Though their minds are the purest and most exalted within cyclic existence, they have not overcome the ignorance of self-grasping,[11] which is the root of samsara, and so, after experiencing bliss for many aeons, eventually their lives end and they are once again reborn in the lower states of cyclic existence. Like the other gods, they consume the merit they have created in the past and make little or no spiritual progress.

The three storeys above ground are called 'the fortunate realms' because the experiences here are relatively pleasant, being caused by the practice of virtue. Below ground are the three lower realms, which are the result of negative physical, verbal, and mental actions. The least painful of these is the animal realm which, in the analogy, is the basement immediately beneath the ground. Included in this realm are all mammals apart from man, as well as birds, fish, insects, worms – the whole animal kingdom. Their minds are characterized by extreme stupidity, without any spiritual awareness, and their lives by fear and brutality.

In the middle basement live the hungry spirits. The principal causes of rebirth here are greed and negative actions motivated by miserliness. The consequence of these actions is extreme poverty. Hungry spirits suffer continuous hunger and thirst which they are unable to satisfy. Their world is a vast desert. If by chance they come across a drop of water or a scrap of food it disappears like a mirage, or transforms into something repulsive such as pus or urine. These appearances are due to their negative karma and lack of merit.

The lowest basement is hell. The beings here experience unrelenting torment. Some hells are a mass of fire; others are desolate regions of ice and darkness. Monsters conjured up by the minds of the hell beings inflict terrible tortures on them. The suffering continues unremittingly for what seems an eternity, but eventually the karma that caused the beings to be born in hell is exhausted and the hell beings die and are reborn elsewhere in samsara.

This is a general picture of samsara. We have been trapped in samsara since beginningless time, wandering meaninglessly, without any freedom or control, from the highest heaven to the deepest hell. Sometimes we dwell in the upper storeys with the gods; sometimes we find ourselves on the ground floor with a human rebirth; but most of the time we are trapped in one of the basements experiencing terrible physical and mental suffering.

Although samsara resembles a prison, there is, however, one door through which we can escape. That door is emptiness, or shunyata in Sanskrit, the ultimate nature of phenomena. By training in the spiritual paths described in this book, we shall eventually find our way to this door, and, stepping through, discover that the house was simply an illusion, the creation of our impure mind. Samsara is not an external prison; it is a prison made by our own mind. It will never end by itself but, by diligently practising the true spiritual path and thereby eliminating our self-grasping and other delusions, we can bring our samsara to an end. Having attained liberation ourselves, we are then in a position to show others how to destroy their mental prison by eradicating their delusions.

*

By practising the twenty-one meditations presented in this book, we will gradually overcome the deluded states of mind that keep us imprisoned in samsara and develop all the qualities needed to attain full enlightenment. The first seven meditations function principally to help us to develop renunciation, the determination to escape from samsara. The next twelve meditations help us to cultivate heartfelt love and compassion for all living beings, and lead us to the realization that we can liberate others from samsara only by attaining enlightenment first. The principal obstacle that prevents us from attaining liberation and enlightenment is self-grasping, a deeply ingrained misconception of the way things exist. The main function of the last two meditations is to counter, and eventually to eradicate, this misconception.

HOW TO MEDITATE

Each of the twenty-one meditation practices has five parts: preparation, contemplation, meditation, dedication, and subsequent practice. The preparatory practices prepare our mind for successful meditation by purifying hindrances caused by our previous negative actions, empowering our mind with merit, and inspiring it with the blessings of the Buddhas and Bodhisattvas. These preparatory practices are performed at the beginning of each meditation session, in conjunction with the short prayers found in the following chapter. It is useful to memorize these prayers. For those who are interested, an explanation of the prayers, as well as instructions on how to set up a shrine and sit in the correct meditation posture, are also given in the following chapter. If our meditation does not seem to be progressing, rather than becoming discouraged we should emphasize these preparatory practices purely and sincerely.

The second part of each practice is contemplation. The purpose of contemplation is to bring to mind the object of placement meditation. This is done by considering various lines of reasoning, contemplating analogies, and reflecting on the scriptures. It is helpful to memorize the contemplations given in each section so that we can meditate without having to refer to the text. The contemplations given here are intended only as guidelines. We should supplement and enrich them with whatever reasons and examples we find helpful.

When, through our contemplations, the object appears clearly, we leave our analytical meditation and concentrate on the object single-pointedly. This single-pointed concentration is the third part, the actual meditation.

When we first start to meditate, our concentration is poor; we are easily distracted and we often lose our object of meditation. Therefore, to begin with, we will probably need to alternate between contemplation and placement meditation many times in each session. For example, if we are meditating on compassion, we begin by contemplating the various sufferings experienced by sentient beings[12] until a strong feeling of compassion arises in our heart. When this feeling arises, we meditate on it single-pointedly. If the feeling fades, or if our mind wanders to another object, we then switch to analytical meditation in order to bring the feeling back to mind. When the feeling has been restored, we once again leave our analytical meditation and hold the feeling with single-pointed concentration.

Both contemplation and meditation serve to acquaint our mind with wholesome objects. The more familiar we are with such objects, the more peaceful our mind becomes. By training in meditation and living in accordance with the insights and resolutions developed during meditation, eventually we shall be able to maintain a peaceful mind continuously, throughout our life. More detailed instructions on the contemplations and on meditation in general can be found in *Joyful Path of Good Fortune*, *Universal Compassion*, and other books on Lamrim.

The fourth part of each practice is dedication. Dedication directs the merit produced by our meditation towards the attainment of Buddhahood. If merit is not dedicated it can easily be destroyed by anger. By reciting the dedication prayer sincerely at the end of each meditation session we ensure that the merit created by meditating is not wasted but acts as a cause for enlightenment.

The fifth part of each meditation practice is the subsequent practice. This consists of advice on how to integrate the meditation into our daily lives. It is important to remember that Dharma practice is not just something we do while we are sitting on our meditation cushion; it should permeate our whole life. It is important that a gulf does not develop between our meditation and our daily life, because the success of our meditation depends upon the purity of our conduct outside the meditation session. We should keep a watch over our mind at all times, applying mindfulness, alertness and conscientiousness,[13] and try to abandon whatever bad habits we may have. Deep experience of Dharma is the result of practical training over a long period of time, both in and out of meditation. Without being in a hurry to see results, we should practise steadily and gently.

To summarize, our mind is like a field. Engaging in the preparatory practices is like preparing the field by removing obstacles caused by past negative actions, making it fertile with merit, and watering it with the blessings of the holy beings. Contemplation and meditation are like sowing good seeds, and dedication and subsequent practice are the methods to ripen our harvest of Dharma realizations.[14]

Lamrim instructions are not given merely for the sake of intellectual understanding of the path to enlightenment. They are instructions that are to be put into practice, given to help us achieve deep experience. By training our mind in these meditations every day, eventually we will achieve perfect realizations of all the Stages of the Path. Until we have reached this stage, we should not tire of listening to oral teachings on Lamrim or reading authentic Lamrim commentaries, and then contemplating and meditating on these instructions. We need continually to expand our understanding of these essential topics and use this new understanding to enhance our regular meditation.

If we genuinely wish to gain experience of the Stages of

the Path we should try to meditate every day. On the first day we can meditate on relying on a Spiritual Guide, on the second day on this precious human rebirth, and so on until we complete the whole cycle in twenty-one days. Then we can begin again. Between sessions we should try to remain mindful of the instructions on subsequent practice. Occasionally, when we have the opportunity, we should do a retreat on Lamrim. A suggested retreat schedule is given in Appendix 2. By practising like this, our whole life is used to further our experience of the Stages of the Path.

The Preparatory Practices

PREPARING FOR MEDITATION

We all have the potential to gain realizations of each of the twenty-one meditation practices in this book. These potentials are like seeds in the field of our mind, and our meditation practice is like cultivating these seeds. However, our meditation practice will be successful only if we make good preparations beforehand.

If we want to cultivate external crops we begin by making careful preparations. First we remove from the soil anything that might obstruct their growth, such as stones and weeds. Secondly, we enrich the soil with compost or fertilizer to give it the strength to sustain growth. Thirdly, we provide warm, moist conditions to enable the seeds to germinate and the plants to grow. In the same way, to cultivate our inner crops of Dharma realizations we must also begin by making careful preparations. Firstly, we must purify our minds in order to eliminate the negative karma we have accumulated in the past for, if we do not purify our negative karma, it will obstruct the growth of Dharma realizations. Secondly, we need to give our mind the strength to support the growth of Dharma realizations by accumulating merit. Thirdly, we need to activate and sustain the growth of Dharma realizations by receiving the blessings of the holy beings.

It is very important to receive blessings. For example, if we are growing outer crops, even if we remove the weeds and fertilize the soil, we will never be able to grow anything if we cannot provide warmth and moisture. These germinate the seeds, sustain the growth of the plants, and finally ripen the crop. In the same way, even if we purify our minds and accumulate merit, it will be difficult to meet with success in our meditations if we do not receive the blessings of the holy beings. Receiving blessings transforms our mind by activating our wholesome potentials, sustaining the growth of our Dharma realizations, and bringing our Dharma practice to completion.

From this we can see that there are three essential preparations for successful meditation: purifying negativities, accumulating merit, and receiving blessings. The brief preparatory practices which now follow contain the essence of these three preparations.

Cleaning the environment

Before we sit down to meditate it is helpful to make sure that the place where we meditate is clean. A clean environment makes the mind clear and fresh. Moreover, during the preparatory practices we will invite the Buddhas, Bodhisattvas and other holy beings to come to our room as a field for accumulating merit, and as a sign of respect we ensure that our room is clean and tidy beforehand.

Setting up a shrine

If possible, we should set up a shrine with representations of Buddha's body, speech and mind. To represent Buddha's body we place a statue or picture in the centre of the shrine. To its right we place a Dharma text, representing Buddha's speech, and to its left we place a stupa, or a picture of a stupa, representing Buddha's mind. Remembering that Buddha's omniscient mind actually enters into these objects, we should feel that we are actually in the presence of the living Buddha and make prostrations and offerings accordingly.

If we like we can set out actual offerings, such as rows of seven water bowls, and anything clean and beautiful, such as flowers, incense, candles, honey, cakes, chocolate or fruit.

More information on setting up a shrine and making offerings can be found in *Joyful Path of Good Fortune*.

The meditation posture

When these preparations are completed we can sit down to meditate. If possible, we should sit in the vajra posture,[15] but if we are unfamiliar with this we can sit in any posture that is comfortable. If we cannot sit cross-legged we can sit in a chair. The most important thing is to have a straight back so that the subtle energies in our body can flow freely and keep our mind alert. Our hands should rest just below the navel, with the right hand above the left and the two thumbs touching.

Calming the mind

Before beginning the actual preparatory prayers we should calm our mind by doing breathing meditation. Breathing naturally, we try to concentrate on our breath without being distracted by conceptual thoughts. As we breathe out we imagine that we exhale all our negativities, obstacles and distracting thoughts in the form of black smoke. As we breathe in we imagine that we inhale the blessings of all the holy beings in the form of pure, white light. We continue with this meditation for a few minutes, or until our mind is calm and peaceful.

The remaining preparatory practices are done in connection with the brief prayers included at the end of this section. The purpose of reciting these prayers is to direct our mind to the particular practices. These will now be briefly explained.

Going for refuge We generate fear of the sufferings of samsara in general, and of rebirth in the lower realms in particular; and then, with strong faith that the Three Jewels have the power to protect us from these sufferings, we go for refuge to Buddha, Dharma, and Sangha while reciting the refuge prayer. The actual practice of going for refuge is explained in Meditation 5.

Generating bodhichitta There are two important things when we meditate: our motivation at the beginning and our dedication at the end. We should begin by generating the motivation of bodhichitta, the wish to attain Buddhahood in order to help all living beings. With this motivation we recite the bodhichitta prayer. Our familiarity with both refuge and bodhichitta will naturally increase as we practise the cycle of twenty-one meditations.

Generating the four immeasurables These are four special states of mind that strengthen our bodhichitta. They are immeasurable love, the wish for all beings to be happy; immeasurable compassion, the wish for all beings to be free from suffering; immeasurable joy, the wish for all beings to attain the everlasting joy of liberation; and immeasurable equanimity, the wish for all beings to be free from unbalanced attitudes such as attachment and anger. They are called 'immeasurables' because we generate these minds while thinking of all sentient beings, whose number is immeasurable.

Visualizing the field for accumulating merit The field for accumulating merit is the assembly of Buddhas, Bodhisattvas and other holy beings in whom we take refuge and to whom we make prostrations, offerings, confession, and so forth. We imagine that they are all in the space before us, with Buddha Shakyamuni, our main object of visualization, in the centre and all the other holy beings around him, like the full moon surrounded by stars. They are called a 'field for accumulating merit' because, by offering the prayer of seven limbs and the mandala to them, we accumulate merit in our minds. At the beginning we should not hope to visualize the whole assembly for accumulating merit. It is sufficient simply to believe that they are all present before us.

Prayer of seven limbs The seven limbs are methods to purify negativity and accumulate merit. They are: prostrating, making offerings, confessing non-virtue, rejoicing in virtue, beseeching the holy beings to remain, requesting Dharma teachings, and dedicating merit. They are called 'limbs' because they support our meditation, which is the main body of our practice. Prostrating, making offerings, rejoicing in virtue, beseeching the holy beings to remain, and requesting Dharma teachings: all accumulate merit; confessing non-virtue purifies negativity; and dedicating our merit prevents our virtue from being destroyed.

To prostrate is to show respect. We can show respect with our body by making physical prostrations, or simply by placing our hands together at our heart; we can show respect with our speech by reciting verses of praise; and we can show respect with our mind by generating faith towards the holy beings. If possible, we should make all three types of prostration together. As well as showing respect, prostrations also serve to reduce our pride.

As already mentioned, we can make offerings by placing seven or more water bowls on our shrine, or by offering anything clean and beautiful, such as flowers, incense, or fruit. By using our imagination we can offer jewelled palaces, gardens, scented bathing pools, even entire universes, all completely pure. The Buddhas and Bodhisattvas have no need of our offerings, but making extensive offerings has a very beneficial effect on our mind, creating a vast amount of merit and countering miserliness.

Confession enables us to purify negative actions committed in the past. If we sincerely contemplate and meditate on karma we will realize that we have already performed innumerable heavy negative actions. Fearing the consequences of these actions, a strong wish to purify them will arise in our mind. In order to purify negative actions we must recognize the faults of these actions and feel regret for having committed them. Regret is not the same as guilt; it is simply a strong wish to purify our mind of the negative energy created by non-virtuous actions. Filled with regret for all the non-virtuous actions we have created, we confess them to the holy beings. In this way we receive the purifying blessings of all Buddhas and Bodhisattvas. With these attitudes of regret and faith, any virtuous actions we engage in act as purification. If we begin every meditation session with sincere confession, the whole session serves to purify our accumulated negativity. To purify completely an unwholesome action we must make a promise not to repeat it. There is little point in confessing our negative actions if we have no intention to refrain from committing them again in the future.

Rejoicing is to appreciate and rejoice in the positive actions of ourselves and others. Rejoicing in virtue increases our virtuous tendencies and overcomes jealousy and competitiveness. It is one of the easiest ways to create a vast amount of merit. Even lying in bed and rejoicing in the virtuous actions of other people is a powerful spiritual practice.

Beseeching our Spiritual Guide and all the other holy beings to remain with us, to guide us and inspire us, helps us to keep a strong connection with our Spiritual Guide in this and future lives.

Requesting the holy beings to turn the Wheel of Dharma, that is, to give Dharma teachings, creates the cause for the Dharma to remain in this world, and ensures that we will meet with the Dharma in our future lives.

Dedication is very important because it directs the merit we accumulate through our meditation practice towards attaining full enlightenment and prevents it from being destroyed by anger or other unwholesome minds such as wrong views. We dedicate by generating a strong mental intention that our merit will become a cause of our enlightenment, for the benefit of all living beings. For those who are interested in practising the seven limbs more elaborately, a detailed commentary is found in the second and third chapters of *Meaningful to Behold*.

Offering the Mandala The mandala offering is a way to offer the entire universe in visualized form. We imagine that the whole universe transforms into a Buddha's Pure Land[16] which we offer to the merit field with the prayer that all living beings may soon come to live in such Pure Lands. To make the mandala offering we visualize that we hold in our hands a vast and circular golden base. In the centre stands Mount Meru. Around this are four island continents, and in the space above are the sun and moon. Everything pure and beautiful is included in the mandala. When we recite the second verse of the mandala offering we offer everything that stimulates our delusions. We imagine that the people and things to which we are attached, as well as those that cause us to develop hatred and confusion, all transform into pure beings and enjoyments, and we offer them to the Three Jewels. By transforming and offering the objects of the three poisons (attachment, hatred and confusion), we remove the basis from which these delusions develop. More detail on offering the mandala can be found in *Joyful Path of Good Fortune* and *Guide to Dakiniland*.

Receiving blessings and purifying After offering the mandala we should imagine that Buddha Shakyamuni and all the other Buddhas and Bodhisattvas are delighted. Smiling at us with the love of a father for his dearest child, Buddha radiates rays of light and nectar from his heart which enter the crown of our head and fill our whole body. This purifies all our hindrances to achieving deep experience of the topic on which we are about to meditate and makes our mind very clear, positive and powerful. We should firmly believe that this happens.

Contemplation and meditation Now that we have purified our mind, accumulated merit and received blessings, we are ready to begin our contemplation and meditation by following the specific instructions given for each meditation.

If, during the course of our meditation, our mind becomes dull or heavy, or if we meet with other difficulties, we should pause from our meditation and make prayers to the holy beings in front of us. We imagine that they answer our prayers with powerful lights and nectars which flow into our body and immediately dispel our obstacles. We then resume our meditation.

These preparations are extremely important for successful meditation. If we wish to spend longer on the preparations, we can recite a slightly more extensive preparatory prayer called 'Essence of Good Fortune', which is found in *Joyful Path of Good Fortune* and *Universal Compassion* (where it is called 'Prayers for the Six Preparations'). If we wish, we can emphasize going for refuge by reciting the refuge prayer hundreds of times, or we can make many mandala offerings, or we can emphasize purification by making prostrations to the Thirty-five Buddhas of Confession. This particular purification practice is explained in *The Bodhisattva Vows*. Sometimes, if we wish, we can devote the entire session to the preparatory practices.

Dedication At the end of our session we imagine that all the holy beings melt into light and dissolve into us through the crown of our head. We feel as if our body, speech and mind have become one with Buddha's body, speech and mind. We then dedicate the merit we have accumulated from practising the preparations, contemplating and meditating to the happiness of all living beings while reciting the dedication prayers.

THE PREPARATORY PRAYERS

Going for refuge

We imagine ourselves and all other sentient beings going for refuge while reciting three times:

I and all sentient beings, until we achieve enlightenment,
Go for refuge to Buddha, Dharma and Sangha.   (3x)

Generating bodhichitta

Through the virtues I collect by giving and other perfections,
May I become a Buddha for the benefit of all.   (3x)

Generating the four immeasurables

May everyone be happy.
May everyone be free from misery.
May no one ever be separated from their happiness.
May everyone have equanimity, free from hatred and
    attachment.

Visualizing the field for accumulating merit

In the space before me is the living Buddha Shakyamuni surrounded by all the Buddhas and Bodhisattvas, like the full moon surrounded by stars.

Prayer of seven limbs

With my body, speech and mind, humbly I prostrate
And make offerings, both set out and imagined.
I confess my wrong deeds from all time,

And rejoice in the virtues of all.
Please stay until samsara ceases,
And turn the Wheel of Dharma for us.
I dedicate all virtues to great enlightenment.

Offering the mandala

The ground sprinkled with perfume and spread with flowers,
The great mountain, four lands, sun and moon
Seen as a Buddhaland and offered thus;
May all beings enjoy such Pure Lands.

I offer without any sense of loss
The objects that give rise to my attachment, hatred, and
    confusion,
My friends, enemies, and strangers, our bodies and
    enjoyments;
Please accept these and bless me to be released directly
    from the three poisons.

IDAM GURU RATNA MANDALAKAM NIRYATAYAMI

Receiving blessings and purifying

From the hearts of all the holy beings, streams of light and
nectar flow down, granting blessings and purifying.

*At this point we begin the actual contemplation and meditation.
After the meditation we dedicate our merit while reciting the
following:*

Dedication prayers

Through the virtues I have collected
By practising the Stages of the Path,

May all living beings find the opportunity
To practise in the same way.

May everyone experience the happiness
Of humans and gods,
And quickly attain enlightenment,
So that samsara is finally extinguished.

PART TWO

———

The Twenty-One
Meditations

Medicine Buddha

The Initial Scope

1. RELYING ON A SPIRITUAL GUIDE

Relying sincerely on a qualified Spiritual Guide is the foundation for all spiritual attainments. In this meditation we generate a strong determination to rely on a Spiritual Guide by considering the many benefits we will experience.

PREPARATION

First we go for refuge, generate a special bodhichitta motivation and complete the other preparatory practices by reciting the brief prayers on pages 21–23.

CONTEMPLATION

We think: 'If I rely sincerely on a Spiritual Guide he or she will lead me along the spiritual path, which is the only way I can solve all my problems and make my life meaningful. I will gradually draw closer to the attainment of full enlightenment. All the Buddhas will be delighted with me. I will be protected from harm caused by humans or non-humans. I will find it easy to abandon delusions and non-virtuous actions. My practical experience of the spiritual path will increase. I will never be born in lower realms. In all my future lives I will meet well-qualified Spiritual Guides. All my wholesome wishes for beneficial conditions within samsara, as well as for liberation and enlightenment,[17] will be fulfilled.'

MEDITATION

We contemplate these benefits until we generate the determination to rely on a Spiritual Guide, sincerely and with strong faith. We meditate on this determination for as long as possible.

DEDICATION

We dedicate all the virtues we have created by engaging in the preparatory practices, contemplating, and meditating, to the welfare of all living beings by reciting the dedication prayers on pages 22 and 23 .

SUBSEQUENT PRACTICE

During the meditation break we should try to please our Spiritual Guide by sincerely putting his instructions into practice. We should improve our faith in him and, in particular, try to prevent negative thoughts towards him. If we wish to practise Dharma but have not yet met a Spiritual Guide, we should be encouraged by the determination made during the meditation to search for a qualified Spiritual Guide who can teach us the Stages of the Path and guide us towards enlightenment.

2. OUR PRECIOUS HUMAN LIFE

By doing this meditation we will come to realize that this human life is very precious because it provides us with a special opportunity to practise Dharma. Once we realize this we will make a strong determination not to waste our life, but use it to practise Dharma purely.

PREPARATION

We go for refuge, generate a special bodhichitta motivation and complete the other preparatory practices as before.

FIRST CONTEMPLATION

Countless sentient beings take rebirth as animals, hungry spirits and hell beings. Because these beings experience continuous, unimaginable sufferings in the lower realms, none of them has the opportunity to practise Dharma. Among those who are born as human beings there are many who have no opportunity to listen to or practise Buddha's teachings. Millions of people live in countries where religion is not tolerated. Some people hold wrong views denying rebirth, the law of karma, or the existence of enlightened beings. Many people are physically or mentally handicapped, or incapacitated by accidents. Others suffer extreme poverty and deprivation, or are caught up in wars or natural disasters. None of these people has the opportunity to follow the spiritual path. Realizing this, we should think, 'Unlike all these poor beings, I am free from all these impediments. I am very fortunate. I have the opportunity to listen to instructions on Buddhadharma[18] and put them into practice. I have faith in these instructions. I have complete mental and physical faculties, and it is easy for me to find all the other conditions that are necessary for practising Dharma.'

King of Clear Knowing

FIRST MEDITATION

We contemplate these points until we generate a feeling of deep appreciation for the preciousness of this human life, seeing that it provides all the conditions necessary for spiritual practice. Thinking, 'I am very fortunate', we then meditate on this feeling single-pointedly.

SECOND CONTEMPLATION

If I use this human life well by practising Dharma, I shall be able to overcome all the problems of this life and protect myself from falling into a lower rebirth in the future. By practising the stages of the path of the intermediate scope I can become free from uncontrolled rebirth and attain the peace of liberation; and by practising the stages of the path of the great scope I can achieve full enlightenment and thereby benefit all sentient beings. This human life is a real wish-fulfilling jewel[19] because it enables me to fulfil my principal wish – to free myself and others from every kind of suffering so that we can experience real happiness. It is only with this human form that I can fulfil this wish.

SECOND MEDITATION

We contemplate these points until we generate the determination: 'I shall use this precious human life to practise Dharma without wasting even a single moment.' We then meditate on this determination single-pointedly.

DEDICATION

We dedicate all the virtues we have created in this meditation practice to the welfare of all living beings by reciting the dedication prayers.

SUBSEQUENT PRACTICE

During the meditation break we try never to lose our appreciation of the preciousness of our human life. If we keep this in mind all the time we will always maintain a happy mind and we will never become discouraged, whatever our external circumstances. Reflecting on the preciousness of our human life will encourage us not to waste our precious time, but to use it to practise the Stages of the Path.

3. DEATH AND IMPERMANENCE

There are three ways in which we can make this human life meaningful: by using it to ensure that we take rebirth as a human or a god in our next life, by using it to attain liberation, or by using it to attain full enlightenment. These attainments depend upon the practice of Dharma, but because we are so attached to worldly activities we do not have a strong wish to practise Dharma. This is our main obstacle. To overcome this obstacle we need to meditate on death.

PREPARATION

We go for refuge, generate a special bodhichitta motivation and complete the other preparatory practices.

CONTEMPLATION

We think: 'I will definitely die. There is no way to prevent my body from finally decaying. Day by day, moment by moment, my life is slipping away. I have no idea when I will die; the time of death is completely uncertain. Many young people die before their parents; some die the moment they are born – there is no certainty in this world. Furthermore, there are so many causes of untimely death. The lives of many strong and healthy people are destroyed by accidents. There is no guarantee that I will not die today.'

MEDITATION

After contemplating these points we mentally repeat over and over again: 'I may die today, I may die today' and concentrate on the feeling it evokes. Eventually we will come to a conclusion: 'Since I will soon have to depart from this world, there is no sense in my becoming attached to worldly enjoyments. Instead, I shall devote my whole life to the practice of Dharma.' We then meditate on this conclusion for as long as we can.

Melodious Ocean of Dharma Proclaimed

DEDICATION

We dedicate all the virtues we have created in this meditation practice to the welfare of all living beings by reciting the dedication prayers.

SUBSEQUENT PRACTICE

During the meditation break we should try to practise Dharma without laziness. Realizing that worldly pleasures are deceptive and that they distract us from using our life in a meaningful way, we should abandon attachment to them. In this way we can eliminate the main obstacle to pure Dharma practice.

Supreme Glory Free from Sorrow

4. THE DANGER OF LOWER REBIRTH

When we die, if the karma that ripens is negative we will take rebirth in one of the lower realms. By meditating on this danger we develop a strong fear of the sufferings of the lower realms. This fear is one of the main causes of going for refuge.

PREPARATION

We go for refuge, generate a special bodhichitta motivation and complete the other preparatory practices.

CONTEMPLATION

When the oil of an oil lamp is exhausted the flame goes out because the flame is produced from the oil, but when our body dies our consciousness is not extinguished because consciousness is not produced from the body. At the time of death our mind has to leave its temporary abode, this present body, and find another, rather like a bird leaving one nest to fly to another. Our mind has no freedom to remain, and no choice about where to go. We are blown to the place of our next rebirth by the winds of our karma. If the karma that ripens at our death time is negative, we will be propelled into a lower rebirth. Heavy negative actions cause rebirth in hell, middling negative actions cause birth as a hungry spirit, and small negative actions cause rebirth in the animal realm.

It is very easy to create heavy negative karma – simply by angrily swotting a mosquito we create the cause to be reborn in hell. In this life, and in our countless previous lives, we have created many heavy negative actions. Unless we have already purified these actions by practising sincere confession their potentialities remain on our mental continuum. Any one of these negative potentialities could ripen when we die. Bearing this in mind, we should ask ourselves: 'If I die today where will I be tomorrow? It is quite possible that I will find myself in the animal realm, among the hungry spirits, or in hell. If someone were to call me a stupid cow I would find it difficult to bear, but what will I do if I really become a cow, or a pig, or a fish?'

MEDITATION

We contemplate the sufferings of the three lower realms, and the danger of being reborn there, until we generate a strong fear of taking rebirth in the lower realms. This feeling of fear is our object of meditation.

DEDICATION

We dedicate all the virtues we have created in this meditation practice to the welfare of all living beings by reciting the dedication prayers.

SUBSEQUENT PRACTICE

During the meditation break we should not forget the danger of taking a lower rebirth. This helps us to maintain mindfulness and conscientiously to avoid non-virtuous actions. We are also inspired to seek refuge in the Three Jewels, the actual protection from suffering.

5. REFUGE PRACTICE

Having developed fear by contemplating the danger of lower rebirth, we now consider how the Three Jewels, Buddha, Dharma and Sangha, have complete power to protect us.

PREPARATION

We go for refuge, generate a special bodhichitta motivation and complete the other preparatory practices.

CONTEMPLATION

All the fears and dangers of samsara, including rebirth in the lower realms, arise from our deluded minds; therefore our real refuge is Dharma, the spiritual realizations that directly protect us from delusions. For example, if we gain a realization of death and impermanence this will help us to reduce our attachment to the things of this life. If we have strong awareness of the inevitability of death and the uncertainty of its time we will naturally value the practice of moral discipline more than the pursuit of transitory sense pleasures, wealth, or power. We will not be tempted to commit non-virtuous actions such as killing, stealing, or sexual misconduct, and so we will not have to experience the unpleasant consequences of such actions. This is how Dharma realizations protect us from suffering. The ultimate Dharma refuge is the realization of emptiness; this permanently pacifies the delusions and frees us once and for all from suffering.

Whereas Dharma is the actual refuge, Buddha is the source of all refuge. He is the supreme Spiritual Guide who shows us the way to achieve Dharma realizations and sustains our Dharma practice by bestowing his blessings. The Sangha are the supreme spiritual friends who support our Dharma practice. They provide conducive conditions, encourage us in our practice, and set a good example for us to follow. Only the Three Jewels have the ability to protect living beings from all suffering.

Stainless Excellent Gold

MEDITATION

By thinking in this way we generate strong conviction that the Three Jewels are the only true objects of refuge, and we develop deep faith in Buddha, Dharma and Sangha. We meditate on this without allowing any doubts to arise.

When we meditate on a mental attitude such as faith, we do not merely think about it and focus on it as if it were separate from our mind, rather we transform our mind into that state and hold it single-pointedly. We should feel as if our mind has merged with an ocean of faith.

After meditating on our faith in the Three Jewels for a short time, we imagine that in front of us is the living Buddha Shakyamuni surrounded by all the Buddhas and Bodhisattvas, like the full moon surrounded by stars. We generate strong conviction that all these holy beings are actually present before us and we focus on them for a while. Dreading rebirth in the lower realms and having deep faith in the Three Jewels, we generate a strong determination to build the foundation of the Dharma Jewel in our mind by relying on the Buddha Jewel and Sangha Jewel. With this motivation we make the following request:

All Buddhas, Bodhisattvas and holy beings,
Please protect me and all sentient beings
From the various sufferings, fears and dangers of
    samsara.
Please bestow your blessings upon our body and mind.

We recite this refuge prayer many times with deep faith in the Three Jewels.

DEDICATION

We dedicate all the virtues we have created in this meditation practice to the welfare of all living beings by reciting the dedication prayers.

SUBSEQUENT PRACTICE

During the meditation break we should practise the twelve commitments of refuge which are explained in detail in Appendix 1. By keeping the refuge commitments, we will strengthen our refuge practice so that it will quickly bear fruit.

6. ACTIONS AND THEIR EFFECTS

Having gone for refuge, our main practice is to observe the laws of karma by abandoning non-virtue and practising virtue. This is the actual method to protect ourselves from rebirth in the lower realms, and the foundation for all other Dharma realizations.

PREPARATION

We go for refuge, generate a special bodhichitta motivation and complete the other preparatory practices.

CONTEMPLATION

The main cause of rebirth in the lower realms is non-virtuous actions, or negative karma. All the suffering we experience in this life, such as disease, poverty, fighting, accidents, harm from humans or non-humans, and so forth, is the result of our past negative actions. If our dearest wishes remain unfulfilled while the things we dislike appear with ease, or if we fail to find good friends, or, having found them, we are soon separated from them, these too are due to the ripening of our past negative karma. Even minor annoyances such as interferences in our daily routine, or the discontent that underlies so much of our lives, are the result of the non-virtuous karma accumulated in previous lives. Conversely, this precious human life, all the happiness experienced by humans and gods, and the attainments of liberation and enlightenment are the result of virtuous actions.

This dependent relationship between actions and their effects, non-virtue causing suffering and virtue causing happiness, is taught by, and based on the perfect knowledge of, the Buddhas. We must believe this because a conviction in the law of karma is the root of future happiness.

King of Melodious Sound

MEDITATION

We contemplate these points until we develop conviction in the truth of karma. Then we make the determination: 'Since I wish to be free from every misfortune and enjoy uninterrupted happiness, I must abandon non-virtuous actions and practise only virtue. In particular, I must abandon the ten non-virtuous actions.'[20] We then make this determination firm by meditating on it with single-pointed concentration.

DEDICATION

We dedicate all the virtues we have created in this meditation practice to the welfare of all living beings by reciting the dedication prayers.

SUBSEQUENT PRACTICE

During the meditation break we should conscientiously avoid even small negative actions and practise whatever virtuous actions we can. In this way we overcome our immediate problems and protect ourselves from future suffering. Practising moral discipline purely makes our human life meaningful. It is the only infallible method to solve our inner problems.

The Intermediate Scope

Due to our self-grasping, since beginningless time we have taken countless rebirths without interruption. This cycle of uninterrupted death, intermediate state and rebirth is known as cyclic existence, or samsara in Sanskrit. As long as we remain trapped within this vicious circle we will experience only suffering.

Going for refuge in the Three Jewels, combined with the practice of pure moral discipline, will free us from the danger of lower rebirth and enable us to obtain a precious human life again in the future. However, even in the human realm we are not free from suffering, and there is no real happiness. We only have to look around us, or read a newspaper, or watch television, to see that human beings experience terrible sufferings.

Wherever we are born in samsara, even in the highest god realm, there is no freedom from suffering. If we succeed in taking rebirth in the fortunate realms it is only like a short holiday. Afterwards we once again have to descend to the lower realms where we experience extreme suffering for inconceivably long periods.

We experience all these sufferings because we are in samsara. If we think deeply about this we will realize that if we want real freedom and real happiness we must escape from samsara. By practising the stages of the path of the intermediate scope we can escape from samsara and achieve permanent inner peace, with complete freedom from all suffering, fears and their causes. This is real liberation, or nirvana.

7. DEVELOPING RENUNCIATION FOR CYCLIC EXISTENCE

The root cause of samsara is self-grasping; therefore to escape from samsara we must cut its root by eradicating self-grasping from our mental continuum. This depends upon training in higher wisdom, which depends upon training in higher concentration, and this, in turn, depends upon training in higher moral discipline. These three higher trainings are so called because they are motivated by renunciation, the wish to escape from samsara. Therefore, our first step in escaping from samsara is to develop a spontaneous realization of renunciation.

We develop renunciation by contemplating the many faults of samsara and generating a strong wish to escape. In the following contemplations we think about the various sufferings experienced in the human realm, but we should bear in mind that the sufferings of other realms are generally far worse.

We may wonder why it is necessary to meditate on sufferings such as birth, ageing, sickness and death, especially since we have already experienced the first and can do nothing to avoid the others. The reason is that by meditating on these sufferings we realize that the very nature of samsaric existence is suffering, and that until we escape from samsara we will have to undergo the same pains in life after life. This induces a strong wish to escape from cyclic existence by abandoning its cause, self-grasping. This wish is renunciation.

PREPARATION

We go for refuge, generate a special bodhichitta motivation and complete the other preparatory practices.

CONTEMPLATION

There now follow seven separate contemplations on the sufferings of samsara, each of which is designed to generate a

Glorious Renown of Excellent Signs

mind of renunciation which is then taken as the object of meditation. It is not necessary to do all the contemplations in each session. Principally we need to contemplate mainly those points that have the greatest impact on our mind and help us to develop renunciation. When renunciation arises in our mind we can then leave the contemplation and proceed to the meditation.

Birth

We have to spend the first nine months of our life cramped inside our mother's womb. At the beginning, the rapid growth of our limbs makes us feel as if we are being stretched out on a rack, and in the later months of pregnancy we feel as if we are squashed inside a small water tank full of filthy liquid. We are extremely sensitive to everything our mother does. For example, if she runs, our fragile body is severely jolted, or if she drinks anything hot it feels like boiling water scalding our skin. During all this time we are completely alone. Our mother does not know the suffering and fear that we experience and, even if she did, she would be powerless to help us.

When we finally emerge from the womb it is like being forced through a narrow crevice between two hard rocks into a harsh and alien world. We have forgotten all we knew in our previous life and have no way of understanding what is now happening to us; it is as if we are blind, deaf and dumb. Our skin is so tender that even the softest clothes feel abrasive. When we are hungry we cannot say, 'I need food', and when we are in pain we cannot say, 'This is hurting me'. The only signs we can make are hot tears and furious gestures. We are completely helpless and have to be taught everything – how to eat, how to sit, how to walk, how to talk.

Ageing

As we grow old our youthful vitality diminishes; we become bent, ugly and burdened with illness. Our eyesight grows weaker and our hearing fails. We cannot derive the same enjoyment from the things we used to enjoy, such as food, drink and sex. We are too weak to play games and we are often too exhausted even for entertainments. When we are young we can travel around the whole world, but when we are old we can hardly walk to our own front gate. We become too weak to engage in many worldly activities, and our spiritual activities are often curtailed. For example, we cannot make many prostrations or go on long pilgrimages. If we do meditation it becomes harder for us to gain realizations because our memory and concentration are weak and we find it difficult to stay awake. Our intellect is less sharp than it was during our youth, so when we try to study it takes much longer to understand things.

Unable to do the work we used to do, or to help others in the way we would like, we begin to feel useless to society and begin to lose our self-respect. We are often neglected by our own children, and we watch helplessly as, one by one, our friends and contemporaries grow sick and die. Inexorably our loneliness deepens. If we did not practise Dharma while we were younger and had the opportunity, we pass our few remaining years with a growing fear of death and a deepening sense of regret for a wasted life.

Sickness

Having been born human, it is almost impossible to escape having to experience sickness in this life. When we fall ill we are like a bird that has been soaring in the sky and is suddenly shot down. When a bird is shot, it falls straight to the ground like a lump of lead and all its glory and power are immediately destroyed. Even a mild illness can be completely incapacitating. We cannot enjoy the food we like or take part in the activities of our friends. We may be told that we must never again eat our favourite food, drink alcohol, or engage in strenuous exercise. If our disease is more serious we may have to undergo painful and possibly risky operations. Should these fail we will be told that the doctors can do nothing to cure us and we have only a short time left to live. If we have not used our life to practise Dharma we will be overcome by fear and regret.

Young people in their prime may be struck down by an incurable degenerative illness and, though they remain alive for many years, they will have to watch themselves slowly deteriorate. Realizing that their most treasured hopes and dreams will never be fulfilled, they may wish they could die sooner. When we hear or read about the horrible diseases experienced by others we must remember the same could happen to us. While we remain in samsara we are never safe from the threat of sickness.

Death

If, during our life, we have worked very hard to accumulate possessions and have become very attached to these, we will experience great suffering when we are separated from them at the time of death. Even now we find it difficult to lend one of our most treasured possessions to someone else, let alone to give it away. No wonder we become so miserable when we realize that in the hands of death we must abandon everything.

When we die we have to part from even our closest friends. We have to leave our husband or wife, even though we may have been together for many years and never spent a day apart. If we are very attached to our friends we will experience great misery at the time of death, but all we will be able to do is to hold their hands. We will not be able to halt the process of death, even if they plead with us not to die. Usually, when we are very attached to someone, we feel jealous if they leave us on our own and spend time with someone else, but when we die we will have to leave our friend with others forever. If we have children we will have to leave them when we die. We will have to leave our Spiritual Guides and all the people who have helped us in this life.

When we die, this body that we have cherished and cared for in so many ways will have to be left behind. It will become mindless like a stone and will be buried in the ground or cremated. If we have not practised Dharma and cultivated wholesome actions, at the time of death we will develop fear and distress, as well as physical pain.

Having to part with what we like

Before the final separation of death we often have to experience temporary separation from the people and things we like. We may have to leave our country where all our friends and relatives live, or we may have to leave the job we like. We may lose our reputation. Many times in this life we have to experience the misery of parting from the people we like, or forsaking and losing the things we find pleasant and attractive, but when we die we have to part forever from all the companions and enjoyments of this life.

Having to encounter what we do not like

We are often forced to live or work with people we find unpleasant, such as those who criticize us for no reason or who continually interfere with our wishes. Sometimes we may find ourselves in very dangerous situations such as a fire or an earthquake, or attacked by a mugger or a rapist. If our country goes to war we may be called up to fight, or be imprisoned if we refuse. Our homes may be bombed and our relatives killed. Our lives are full of less extreme situations which we find annoying. On holiday it rains, but back in the office the heat is stifling. Our business fails, or we lose our jobs, or we use up all our savings. We argue with our partner, our children cause us many worries, and old friends suddenly turn against us. Whatever we do, something always seems to go wrong. Even in our Dharma practice we continually meet obstacles. When we sit down to meditate we are distracted by outside noise, or the telephone rings, or someone calls to see us. Sometimes it seems that, even though we have been practising for years, our delusions are stronger than ever. Even though we try so hard to be considerate, sometimes our family or our friends become unhappy about our Dharma practice. It is as if we are living in a thorn bush – whenever we adjust ourselves to make ourselves more comfortable, the thorns only pierce us more deeply. In samsara, aggravation and frustration are the natural state of affairs.

Failing to satisfy our desires

We have countless desires; many cannot be fulfilled at all and others, when fulfilled, do not bring us the satisfaction we hoped for. Many people are unable to satisfy even modest desires for the basic necessities of life such as adequate food, clothing, shelter, companionship, tolerable work, or a degree of personal freedom. Unfortunately, even if these basic needs are met, our desires do not end there. Soon we need a car, a more luxurious home, a better-paid job. In the past a simple holiday by the seaside may have been sufficient, but our expectations continually increase and now we need expensive, foreign holidays.

Ambition and competitiveness are a common cause of dissatisfaction. The ambitious schoolchild cannot rest content until he or she comes top of the class, nor the businessman until he has made his fortune. Clearly not everyone can come top; for one person to win, others must lose. But even the winners are rarely satisfied for long; their ambition drives them on until they too are beaten, worn out or dead.

Another reason why we fail to satisfy all our desires is that they are often contradictory. For example, we may want both worldly success and a simple life, or fame and privacy, or rich food and a slim figure, or excitement and security. We may demand our own way all the time and still expect to be popular, or we may wish for Dharma realizations yet still covet a good reputation and material wealth.

Our desires often involve other people and this creates special complications. Many relationships break up because of unrealistic expectations and desires.

We seek perfection – the perfect society, the perfect home, the perfect partner – but perfection cannot be found in samsara. Samsara promises much but can never deliver the satisfaction we long for. It is not possible for impure, transient objects to provide the lasting joy we seek. This can be attained only by thoroughly purifying our mind. Though ignorance is the fundamental cause, worldly desires are the fuel that perpetuates the fire of samsara; therefore it is essential to reduce our worldly desires by recognizing their disadvantages.

MEDITATION

By contemplating these seven kinds of suffering we will develop the thought, 'I have experienced these sufferings over and over again in the past and, if I do not attain liberation, I shall have to experience them over and over again in the future. Therefore I must become free from samsara.' When this thought arises clearly and definitely in our mind we do placement meditation.

DEDICATION

We dedicate all the virtues we have created in this meditation practice to the welfare of all living beings by reciting the dedication prayers.

SUBSEQUENT PRACTICE

Throughout the meditation break we should maintain the wish to attain liberation from samsara. When we meet with difficult circumstances we should use these to remind ourself of the disadvantages of samsara. When things are going well, we should not be deceived but recall that samsaric pleasures are short-lived and they ensnare us if we become attached to them.

The Great Scope

The wish to escape from samsara should be maintained both day and night. It is the main path to liberation and the basis of more advanced realizations. However, we should not be content with seeking merely our own liberation, we need also to consider the welfare of other sentient beings. There are countless beings trapped in the prison of samsara experiencing an unlimited variety of sufferings. Whereas each one of us is just one single person, other people are countless in number; therefore the happiness of others is much more important than our own happiness. For this reason we must enter the Mahayana path, the supreme method to benefit all sentient beings.

8. DEVELOPING EQUANIMITY

Our attitudes towards others are normally unbalanced. When we see a friend, or someone we find particularly attractive, we are pleased; when we meet an enemy, or an unattractive person, a feeling of dislike automatically arises; and when we meet a stranger, or someone we find neither attractive nor unattractive, our mind remains indifferent to them. Such unbalanced attitudes are the main obstacle to developing unbiased love, compassion and bodhichitta, which are the essential realizations of the Mahayana. For as long as we have these attitudes our mind will be like a rocky field which cannot support the growth of Mahayana realizations. Our first task, therefore, is to free our mind from these unbalanced attitudes and develop a genuine equanimity towards all living beings.

PREPARATION

We go for refuge, generate a special bodhichitta motivation and complete the other preparatory practices.

CONTEMPLATION

We should think that in previous lives the person who is now our friend was often our enemy, while our present enemy has often been our closest friend. Even within one short life, friends quickly turn into enemies and enemies turn into friends. There is no certainty. Moreover, in the past we have been close to those we now regard as strangers, and there will come a time when we will become estranged from those we now feel close to. Therefore, there is no sense in our being attached to some and feeling aversion or indifference towards others. By thinking in this way we can give up these unbalanced attitudes of attachment, aversion and indifference and cultivate instead a feeling of warmth for all living beings.

Avalokiteshvara

MEDITATION

By contemplating these points we arrive at three resolutions:

1 I shall free my mind from unbalanced attitudes.
2 I shall not feel attachment, aversion, or indifference towards any living being.
3 I shall develop and maintain a warm and friendly attitude towards all living beings equally.

We meditate single-pointedly on these three resolutions for as long as possible.

DEDICATION

We dedicate all the virtues we have created in this meditation practice to the welfare of all living beings by reciting the dedication prayers.

SUBSEQUENT PRACTICE

We should maintain these three resolutions day and night, keeping in our heart a warm feeling towards everyone we meet or think about. If we do this there will be no basis for the problems of attachment or anger. Our mind will remain at peace all the time.

Manjushri

9. RECOGNIZING THAT ALL SENTIENT BEINGS ARE OUR MOTHERS

Having generated equanimity, we now need to generate love, compassion and bodhichitta. These depend upon first generating affectionate love for all sentient beings. In order to generate affectionate love, we begin by contemplating how all sentient beings are our mothers.

PREPARATION

We go for refuge, generate a special bodhichitta motivation and complete the other preparatory practices.

CONTEMPLATION

Since it is impossible to find a beginning to our mental continuum, it follows that we have taken innumerable rebirths in the past. If we have had countless rebirths, we must have had countless mothers. Where are all these mothers now? They are all the sentient beings alive today.

It is incorrect to reason that our mothers of former lives are no longer our mothers just because a long time has passed since they actually cared for us. If our present mother were to die today, would she cease to be our mother? No, we would still regard her as our mother and pray for her happiness. The same is true of all our previous mothers – they died, yet they still remain our mothers. It is only because of the changes in our external appearance that we do not recognize each other.

In our daily life we see many different sentient beings, both human and non-human. We regard some as friends, some as enemies, and most as strangers. These distinctions are made by our mistaken minds; they are not verified by valid cognition.[21] As a result of the different karmic relationships we have had in the past, some sentient beings now appear to us to be attractive, some unattractive, and others neither particularly attractive nor unattractive. We tend to assent to these appearances unquestioningly, as if they were really true. We believe that those who now appear pleasant are intrinsically pleasant people, while those we find unattractive are actually unpleasant. This way of thinking is clearly incorrect. Rather than following such mistaken minds it would be better to regard all sentient beings as our mothers. Whoever we meet, we should think: 'This person is my mother.' In this way we will feel equally warm towards all living beings.

If we regard all living beings as our mothers, we will find it easy to develop pure love and compassion. Our everyday relationships will become pure and stable, and we will naturally avoid negative actions such as killing or harming living beings. Since it is so beneficial to view all sentient beings as our mothers, we should do so without hesitation.

MEDITATION

We contemplate in this way until we develop the conviction that all beings are our mothers. Then we meditate on this conviction single-pointedly to make it firm.

DEDICATION

We dedicate all the virtues we have created in this meditation practice to the welfare of all living beings by reciting the dedication prayers.

SUBSEQUENT PRACTICE

In between sessions we should regard everyone we meet as our mother. This applies even to animals and insects, as well as our enemies. Instead of identifying people as friends, enemies or strangers, we should try to view them all equally as being our mother. In this way the harmful attitudes of hatred, attachment and indifference will be overcome.

10. REMEMBERING THE KINDNESS OF
SENTIENT BEINGS

Having become convinced that all sentient beings are our mothers, we now contemplate their kindness in order to generate a feeling of affectionate love towards them. In this meditation we begin by contemplating the immense kindness we have received from each sentient being when they were our mother, and then we contemplate and meditate on the kindness they have shown us at other times.

PREPARATION

We go for refuge, generate a special bodhichitta motivation and complete the other preparatory practices.

CONTEMPLATION

When we were conceived, had our mother not wanted to keep us in her womb she could have had an abortion. If she had done so we would not now have this human form. Through her kindness she allowed us to stay in her womb, and so we now enjoy a human life and experience all its advantages. When we were a baby, had we not received her constant care and attention we would certainly have had an accident and could now be handicapped, crippled or blind. Fortunately our mother did not neglect us; day and night she gave us her loving care, regarding us as more important than herself. She saved our life many times each day. During the night she allowed her sleep to be interrupted and during the day she forfeited her usual pleasures. She had to leave her job, and when her friends went out to enjoy themselves she had to stay behind. She spent all her money on us, giving us the best food and the best clothes she could afford. She taught us how to eat, how to walk, how to talk. Thinking of our future welfare she did her best to ensure that we received a good education. Owing to her kindness we are free from physical handicaps and are able to study whatever

Vajrapani

we choose. It is principally through the kindness of our mother that we now have the opportunity to practise Dharma and eventually achieve enlightenment.

There is no one who has not been our mother at some time in our previous lives, and when we were their child they treated us with the same kindness as our present mother has treated us in this life. Therefore all sentient beings are very kind.

The kindness of sentient beings is not limited to the times when they have been our mother. All the time our day-to-day needs are provided through the kindness of others. We brought nothing with us from our former life, yet as soon as we were born we were given a home, food, clothes and everything we needed – all provided by the kindness of others. Everything we now enjoy has been provided through the generosity of other beings, past or present.

We are able to make use of many things with very little effort on our own part. If we consider facilities such as roads, cars, trains, aeroplanes, ships, restaurants, hotels, libraries, hospitals, shops, money and so on, it is clear that many people worked very hard to provide these things. Even though we may make little or no contribution towards the provision of these facilities, they are all available for us to use. This shows the great kindness of others.

Both our general education and our spiritual training are provided by others. All our Dharma realizations, from our very first insights up to our eventual attainment of liberation and enlightenment, will be achieved in dependence upon the kindness of others.

MEDITATION

We contemplate the great kindness of mother sentient beings until we develop a deep sense of gratitude. We then meditate on this feeling single-pointedly.

DEDICATION

We dedicate all the virtues we have created in this meditation practice to the welfare of all living beings by reciting the dedication prayers.

SUBSEQUENT PRACTICE

Throughout all our activities we should maintain the recognition that all beings are very kind to us. This special way of viewing sentient beings will prevent us from becoming involved in arguments or from criticizing others. The realizations of love, compassion and bodhichitta will easily be attained.

11. EQUALIZING SELF AND OTHERS

To equalize self and others is to cherish others as much as we cherish ourselves. Until now we have cherished only ourselves. The aim of this meditation is to share our feeling of cherishing so that we come to cherish ourselves and all sentient beings equally.

PREPARATION

We go for refuge, generate a special bodhichitta motivation and complete the other preparatory practices.

CONTEMPLATION

We think: 'There are three correct reasons why I should cherish myself and others equally:

1 All sentient beings have shown me great kindness in both this and previous lives.
2 Just as I wish to be free from suffering and experience only happiness, so do all other beings. In this respect I am no different from any other being; we are all equal.
3 I am only one, whereas others are countless, so how can I cherish myself alone while I neglect to cherish others? My happiness and suffering are insignificant when compared with the happiness and suffering of all other sentient beings.'

MEDITATION

We contemplate these three reasons until a determination to cherish ourselves and others equally arises strongly in our mind. We then meditate on this for as long as possible.

DEDICATION

We dedicate all the virtues we have created in this meditation practice to the welfare of all living beings by reciting the dedication prayers.

Maitreya

SUBSEQUENT PRACTICE

Whenever we meet someone, or think of someone, we should remember the determination we made in the meditation session and cherish them sincerely. We should feel affectionate love for all living beings and always value their happiness and freedom. By training in this way many of the problems we experience in daily life will disappear, because most of our problems arise from regarding ourselves as more important than others.

Samantabhadra

12. THE DISADVANTAGES OF SELF-CHERISHING

We usually regard ourselves as especially precious and important, and feel that our own happiness matters most. This attitude, which is known as 'self-cherishing', is a great obstacle to developing great compassion and bodhichitta. In this meditation we generate a strong determination to overcome our self-cherishing by considering its many faults and disadvantages.

PREPARATION

We go for refuge, generate a special bodhichitta motivation and complete the other preparatory practices.

CONTEMPLATION

Motivated by self-cherishing we perform many negative actions – physical, verbal and mental. As a result of these negative actions we experience suffering and misfortune. All suffering, all fear, and all unfulfilled wishes are the result of negative karma, and all negative karma arises from self-cherishing.

If we hear even the slightest criticism we immediately feel pain because our self-cherishing mind wishes to hear only those things that make us feel comfortable. All our unhappiness, depression and mental discomfort comes from self-cherishing.

If a mother sentient being such as a poor, hungry mouse were to come into our room searching for food, we would probably become unhappy, and instead of generating compassion we might even become angry. This is because our self-cherishing regards only ourselves as important and has no wish to benefit others.

It is generally assumed that self-cherishing is necessary for survival, and that it is only because we cherish ourselves that we look after ourselves at all. On the surface this seems to be true, but if we think more deeply, taking into account the law of karma, we will realize that the opposite is the case. In actual fact, the self-cherishing we harbour in our hearts is responsible for all our problems and constantly destroys our well-being, even threatening our very survival. For example, some people become so disappointed or angry when their wishes are not fulfilled that they kill themselves. Such anger or despair arises only from strong attachment to one's own happiness, so indirectly self-cherishing is responsible even for suicide. Nothing causes us greater harm than this demon of self-cherishing; it is the source of all negativity and all misfortune.

We do not need self-cherishing in order to look after ourselves, or to survive. If we regard our bodies as being in the service of others, we can eat, wash, work, rest and so on without self-cherishing. Moreover, people who genuinely love others and have an unselfish, undemanding disposition are generally well-liked and readily receive assistance from others.

MEDITATION

We contemplate these points until we develop a strong determination to abandon our self-cherishing. Then we meditate single-pointedly on that determination.

DEDICATION

We dedicate all the virtues we have created in this meditation practice to the welfare of all living beings by reciting the dedication prayers.

SUBSEQUENT PRACTICE

We should be ever mindful of the faults of self-cherishing and, by repeatedly recalling the determination we made in meditation, we should try gradually to abandon it. Whenever we experience difficulties or suffering we should not blame other people or the external situation, rather we should remember that ultimately all our problems arise from self-cherishing. Therefore, when things go wrong we should blame only our self-cherishing mind. By practising in this way, our self-cherishing, the root of all faults, will gradually diminish and eventually it will cease altogether.

Kshitigarbha

13. THE ADVANTAGES OF CHERISHING OTHERS

Previously we generated affectionate love for all mother sentient beings. On the basis of this we now need to generate cherishing love, a mind that regards all living beings as important and feels them to be very special. In this meditation we generate a strong determination to cherish others by contemplating the many advantages of so doing.

PREPARATION

We go for refuge, generate a special bodhichitta motivation and complete the other preparatory practices as before.

CONTEMPLATION

If we think clearly we will realize that all our present and future happiness depends upon our cherishing others. How is this? In our past lives, because we cherished others, we practised moral discipline such as refraining from killing or harming others, abandoning stealing from them, and so forth. Sometimes, out of fondness for them, we practised giving and patience. As a result of these positive actions we have now obtained this precious human life. Moreover, because sometimes in the past we helped others and gave them protection, we ourselves now receive help and enjoy pleasant conditions.

If we sincerely practise cherishing others we will experience many benefits in this and future lives. The immediate effect will be that many of our problems such as those that arise from anger, jealousy and so forth will disappear, and our minds will become calm and peaceful. Since we will act in a considerate way, we will please others and not become involved in quarrels or disputes. If we cherish others we will be concerned not to harm them, so we will naturally avoid negative actions. Instead, we will practise positive actions such as love, patience and generosity and thus create the cause to gain a precious human life in the future.

If we make cherishing others our main practice, we will gradually develop very special minds of great compassion and bodhichitta, and as a result we will eventually come to enjoy the ultimate happiness of full enlightenment.

MEDITATION

We contemplate these points until we arrive at the decision: 'I must always cherish other beings because this precious mind of love will bring happiness to myself and others.' We then hold this thought and meditate on it single-pointedly for as long as possible.

DEDICATION

We dedicate all the virtues we have created in this meditation practice to the welfare of all living beings by reciting the dedication prayers.

SUBSEQUENT PRACTICE

During the meditation break we should continue to keep in mind the advantages of cherishing others and gradually improve our consideration, respect and love for them.

14. EXCHANGING SELF WITH OTHERS

Exchanging self with others means to change the object of our cherishing so that we give up self-cherishing and cherish only others.

PREPARATION

We go for refuge, generate a special bodhichitta motivation and complete the other preparatory practices.

CONTEMPLATION

Since beginningless time we have cherished only ourselves. So strong has been our self-cherishing that we have never forgotten our own welfare for a moment, even during sleep. Again and again this attitude has caused us to create the karma to be reborn in samsara and experience relentless suffering.

Buddha himself, and many of his followers, have understood the disadvantages of self-cherishing and the advantages of cherishing others. They have realized that the main cause of the ultimate happiness of Buddhahood is exchanging self with others. Therefore they have abandoned self-cherishing, and have come to regard the happiness of all other living beings as supremely important, dedicating all their actions to the welfare of others. The result is that they have attained full enlightenment and have been able to rescue many sentient beings from the sufferings of cyclic existence.

MEDITATION

We contemplate these points until we achieve a deep understanding of them. Finally we come to the conclusion: 'I must abandon self-cherishing and cherish only others because self-cherishing is the source of all suffering and the root of samsara, and cherishing others is the source of all happiness and

Sarvanivaranaviskambini

the root of liberation and full enlightenment.' When this determination arises in our mind we meditate on it single-pointedly.

DEDICATION

We dedicate all the virtues we have created in this meditation practice to the welfare of all living beings by reciting the dedication prayers.

SUBSEQUENT PRACTICE

By remaining mindful of the determination made in meditation we should try not to follow our instinctive self-cherishing but instead try to cherish others. When we are familiar with exchanging self with others we will become like the great Tibetan Bodhisattva Geshe Langri Tangpa,[22] who was able to accept happily any pain or difficulty such as illness, loss, or criticism, and to offer all his success and good conditions to others.

Akashagarbha

15. GREAT COMPASSION

Having developed cherishing love for all sentient beings, we now contemplate their suffering so that we can generate compassion for them. For this meditation we imagine that our present parents are beside us, and that they are surrounded by all sentient beings of the six realms. To help us visualize them we can imagine them all in human aspect, but we should remember that in reality they are beings of the six realms experiencing their own particular sufferings.

PREPARATION

We go for refuge, generate a special bodhichitta motivation and complete the other preparatory practices.

CONTEMPLATION

None of these poor beings around me wants to suffer. They all long to be free, but they do not know how to escape. They are confused about the real causes of suffering, so they cannot find the means to abandon it. Out of their ignorance they continually perform actions that cause them to be reborn in samsara. It seems as if their misery has no end.

Because they have taken rebirth in samsara, all these beings are experiencing continuous suffering. For example, the human beings are experiencing unbearable human suffering. Without any choice they have to experience the sufferings of birth, ageing, sickness and death. Again and again they have to part with what they like and encounter what they do not like. They are never able to satisfy their desires but experience constant disappointment and frustration.

If we recall our contemplations on these seven sufferings from the meditation on renunciation and now apply them to others, we will see that all human beings are experiencing constant suffering. We can increase our awareness of human suffering by recalling tragedies that we ourselves have witnessed, read about, or seen on television.

The suffering of animals is a hundred times worse than human suffering, and the suffering experienced by hungry spirits is even worse. The most severe and long-lasting suffering is experienced by hell beings.

Although the gods and demi-gods generally enjoy better physical conditions than do humans, even they are not free from mental suffering, and in the future they will once again have to experience the immense sufferings of the lower realms.

MEDITATION

We contemplate these points until there arises in our mind a strong feeling of compassion for all sentient beings. We generate the compassionate wish: 'How wonderful it would be if all living beings were free from suffering', and meditate on this wish for as long as possible.

DEDICATION

We dedicate all the virtues we have created in this meditation practice to the welfare of all living beings by reciting the dedication prayers.

SUBSEQUENT PRACTICE

During the meditation break we should try to maintain a compassionate heart day and night. Whenever we see or hear of others' suffering we should try to strengthen our compassion. We must also try to help in practical ways wherever possible. For example, we can rescue animals whose lives are in danger, comfort those who are distressed, or relieve the pain of those who are sick.

16. TAKING

Having developed the compassionate wish for all sentient beings to be freed from their suffering, we now need to realize that it is not enough merely to wish for this to happen; we must personally take on the responsibility of making it happen.

PREPARATION

We go for refuge, generate a special bodhichitta motivation and complete the other preparatory practices.

CONTEMPLATION

We begin by generating the superior intention: 'I myself will liberate all beings from their suffering.' Motivated by this superior intention we pray: 'May all the suffering, fears and obstacles of every sentient being ripen on me, and may they thereby be freed from all problems.' We imagine that all their sufferings, fears and obstacles gather in the aspect of black smoke which dissolves into our heart, destroying our self-cherishing mind and freeing all sentient beings from their suffering.

MEDITATION

We develop strong conviction that all sentient beings have actually been released from their suffering and that our self-cherishing mind has been completely destroyed. With this conviction we generate a feeling of great joy. We take this feeling of joy as our object of meditation and hold it with single-pointed concentration for as long as possible.

DEDICATION

We dedicate all the virtues we have created in this meditation practice to the welfare of all living beings by reciting the dedication prayers.

Atisha

SUBSEQUENT PRACTICE

During the meditation break we should put our compassionate intention into practice by alleviating others' suffering whenever we can. In this way we increase both our compassion and our merit. We should patiently accept whatever misfortune befalls us and use our own suffering as an example to help us develop sympathy for others. By practising in these ways our self-cherishing will gradually diminish and we will develop the courage actually to take on the suffering of others.

Dromtönpa

17. WISHING LOVE

In this meditation we once again imagine ourselves surrounded by all living beings, with our parents closest to us.
We then recall from our previous meditations the love that
cherishes all beings equally. With this mind we contemplate
how all the beings around us have no real happiness. This
naturally gives rise to the wish for them to find pure happiness. This wish is called 'wishing love'.

PREPARATION

We go for refuge, generate a special bodhichitta motivation
and complete the other preparatory practices.

CONTEMPLATION

Although all these beings desire real happiness, they do not
know how to obtain it. Instead of engaging in actions that
cause real happiness, they destroy whatever merit they have
by getting angry, by holding wrong views, or by committing
other negative actions.

No one in samsara enjoys real happiness. The happiness
experienced by samsaric beings is simply worldly pleasure,
which in reality is the suffering of change.[23] In samsara all
pleasures are short-lived and eventually change into pain.
For example, the worldly pleasure we experience in ordinary
relationships is not real happiness, but a temporary diminish-
ment of our loneliness. Sooner or later, problems arise in our
relationship, or it comes to an end. Our pleasures never last.

We generally assume that rich people must experience
true happiness because they can enjoy all the pleasures and
luxuries we would like to enjoy, but the pleasure they experience is, in reality, merely a temporary reduction of the suffering of discontent which arises from their unfulfilled desires.

MEDITATION

We contemplate these points until we generate a sincere wish: 'How wonderful it would be if all beings obtained true happiness!' We take this mind of wishing love as our object of meditation and hold it single-pointedly.

DEDICATION

We dedicate all the virtues we have created in this meditation practice to the welfare of all living beings by reciting the dedication prayers.

SUBSEQUENT PRACTICE

During the meditation break we should maintain wishing love day and night, by constantly reminding ourselves that these sentient beings whom we cherish so much have no true happiness. When our hearts are filled with pure love we cannot be disturbed by anger or jealousy.

18. GIVING

Having generated the wish for all sentient beings to be happy, we now train in actually giving them happiness.

PREPARATION

We go for refuge, generate a special bodhichitta motivation and complete the other preparatory practices.

CONTEMPLATION

We begin by generating the intention: 'Since I wish for all beings to enjoy true happiness, I must act to make this really happen.' With this motivation we imagine that our body transforms into a wish-fulfilling jewel from which light radiates and illuminates all six realms. From this light humans receive whatever they desire, animals are freed from danger, hungry spirits receive food and drink, beings in the cold hells receive warmth, and a cooling breeze refreshes those in the hot hells. Demi-gods are granted protection, and gods are blessed with uncontaminated happiness.

MEDITATION

We generate strong conviction that, as a result of our practice of giving, all sentient beings experience an uncontaminated happiness and are completely satisfied. With this conviction we generate a special feeling of joy. We then meditate on this feeling for as long as possible.

Once we have become familiar with the practices of taking and giving as explained here, we can combine them by mounting them on the breath. To do this we must have the correct motivation of compassion and love for all beings. Breathing naturally, we imagine that when we breathe in we inhale, in the form of black smoke, all the suffering, delusions and negative karma of all sentient beings. This black smoke

Geshe Potowa

enters through our nostrils and descends to our heart where it completely destroys our self-cherishing mind. As a result, our mind transforms into uncontaminated bliss and our body becomes the pure body of a Buddha. As we breathe out we exhale white light which blesses the minds of all sentient beings and grants them whatever they desire or need. We repeat this visualization with each inhalation and exhalation.

Since there is quite a lot to visualize in a short space of time, it is difficult to do this practice if we are not already familiar with the basic meditations on taking and giving. Once these are mastered, however, this practice is an exceptionally powerful method for developing and increasing our compassion, love, and bodhichitta.

The breath and the mind are closely related. If the breath is harnessed for wholesome purposes it will gradually become pure, and as a result our mind will gradually become peaceful. Since we breathe all the time, if we use this method to keep our breath pure we will easily be able to maintain peaceful and wholesome states of mind all the time.

More elaborate instructions on taking and giving can be found in *Universal Compassion*.

DEDICATION

We dedicate all the virtues we have created in this meditation practice to the welfare of all living beings by reciting the dedication prayers.

SUBSEQUENT PRACTICE

During the meditation break we should try to practise giving material things, giving Dharma, and giving fearlessness.[24] Whenever we can, we should try to be of service to others. We should also make prayers and dedicate our merit so that all sentient beings obtain pure happiness. In this way our wishing love as well as our merit will increase.

Je Tsongkhapa

19. BODHICHITTA

The nine meditations from equanimity to giving are the actual methods to develop bodhichitta. In general, there are two methods for developing bodhichitta: the method of the sevenfold cause and effect,[25] and the method of equalizing and exchanging self with others.[26] The system presented here is a synthesis of these two traditions. Through improving our experience of these meditations we generate a special bodhichitta. In particular, the superior intention generated through taking and giving directly induces an especially powerful bodhichitta. This is defined as a primary mind[27] spontaneously wishing to achieve Buddhahood for the sake of all sentient beings that is motivated by the special superior intention arising from exchanging self with others.

PREPARATION

We go for refuge, generate a special bodhichitta motivation and complete the other preparatory practices.

CONTEMPLATION

We recall the superior intention generated in the meditation on taking and think: 'I have assumed responsibility for liberating all sentient beings from suffering, but how can I do this without first attaining enlightenment myself? Only a Buddha has the ability to protect all living beings and bestow on them uncontaminated bliss. Therefore, in order to fulfil my wish to free others from their suffering, I must become a Buddha.'

MEDITATION

When, by contemplating in this way, we arrive at the conclusion: 'I must attain Buddhahood for the benefit of all', we hold it single-pointedly for as long as possible. If the thought begins to fade we renew it by repeating the contemplation.

DEDICATION

We dedicate all the virtues we have created in this meditation practice to the welfare of all living beings by reciting the dedication prayers.

SUBSEQUENT PRACTICE

We should try to maintain bodhichitta day and night. In particular, we should try to ensure that whatever actions we undertake are motivated by bodhichitta. In this way all our actions become powerful causes of Buddhahood.

Having gained some experience of bodhichitta, we should bring it to completion by practising the three higher trainings of the Mahayana: training in the perfection of moral discipline by keeping the Bodhisattva vows purely, training in the perfection of mental stabilization by striving to attain tranquil abiding, and training in the perfection of wisdom by developing superior seeing.

20. TRANQUIL ABIDING

To release our mind from self-grasping, the root of all delusions, we need a direct realization of emptiness. This depends upon tranquil abiding. Without tranquil abiding our mind is unstable, like a candle flame exposed to the wind, and so we are not able to realize clearly and directly subtle objects such as emptiness. It is not just the direct realization of emptiness that depends upon tranquil abiding; we also need tranquil abiding to achieve pure clairvoyance, miracle powers, and spontaneous realizations of renunciation and bodhichitta.

In general, whenever we experience pure concentration on any of the objects of the twenty-one meditations our mind abides in a tranquil state, free from distractions; this is the function of pure concentration. However, actual tranquil abiding is a special concentration that is attained by completing the training in the nine levels of concentration – known as 'the nine mental abidings' – and which is conjoined with a special bliss of mental and physical suppleness.[28] In order to train in tranquil abiding we first need to choose an object of meditation. We can use any one of the objects of the twenty-one meditations. If we choose an object such as equanimity, love, compassion, or bodhichitta, we first transform our mind into that particular state of mind by using the appropriate contemplations, and then we hold that state of mind with single-pointed concentration. If we choose an object such as emptiness, impermanence, or the preciousness of this human life, we first attain a clear mental image of the object by relying on the appropriate contemplations, and then we concentrate single-pointedly on that image.

When we are training in tranquil abiding we have to overcome five major faults: laziness, forgetfulness, sinking and excitement, non-application, and application. To do this we have to train in the eight antidotes: faith, aspiration, effort, suppleness, mindfulness, alertness, application, and non-application. These are explained in detail in *Joyful Path of Good Fortune*.

Je Phabongkhapa

The instructions that follow explain how to begin to train in tranquil abiding using great compassion as the object. If you choose a different object you can modify the instructions accordingly.

PREPARATION

We go for refuge, generate a special bodhichitta motivation and complete the other preparatory practices.

CONTEMPLATION

By recalling our previous meditations, we first bring to mind the love that cherishes all other living beings. With this mind we then think deeply about the suffering experienced by these poor beings. When, as a result of these contemplations, a strong feeling of compassion arises in our mind, we have found our object of tranquil abiding meditation.

MEDITATION

Having transformed our mind into compassion, we now stop contemplating and hold this mind with strong concentration. This is the first of the nine mental abidings. When the object fades, or our mind wanders to another object, we return to the contemplations in order to bring the object back to mind. Then once again we discontinue our contemplations and hold the object with single-pointed concentration. We continue in this way, alternating between contemplation and meditation, for the rest of the session.

We continue to improve our concentration in this way until we are able to remain concentrated on our object for five minutes. At this point we shall have advanced to the second mental abiding. By gradually improving our concentration further we will progress through the nine mental abidings and eventually attain tranquil abiding itself. At this point, although we will still have the body of a human being, our mind will be the mind of a form realm god.

DEDICATION

We dedicate all the virtues we have created in this meditation practice to the welfare of all living beings by reciting the dedication prayers.

SUBSEQUENT PRACTICE

The principal practice during the meditation break is carefully to observe pure moral discipline by relying on mindfulness and conscientiousness. In this way we avoid distracting entanglements that will obstruct our training in tranquil abiding. Again and again we should think about the benefits of attaining tranquil abiding in order to increase our enthusiasm for the practice, and to improve our understanding we should read authentic instructions on tranquil abiding such as those found in *Joyful Path of Good Fortune* and *Meaningful to Behold*.

Once we have achieved the fourth mental abiding, we are ready to do a strict retreat on tranquil abiding. In some cases, at this stage it is possible to achieve actual tranquil abiding within six months. For our retreat on tranquil abiding to be successful we need to find a suitable place which is very quiet and has all the necessary conditions. We must have few desires and be able to remain content all the time. During the retreat we should refrain from worldly activities and keep moral discipline purely, thereby reducing distracting conceptions. In brief, we must free ourselves from all obstacles to developing concentration and obtain all conducive internal and external conditions.

21. SUPERIOR SEEING

Superior seeing is a wisdom achieved after the attainment of tranquil abiding that is held by a special bliss of suppleness produced by analyzing the nature of the object. The principal object of superior seeing is emptiness; therefore, in this section we emphasize meditation on emptiness.

Emptiness is not nothingness, but the lack of inherent existence. Inherent existence is mistakenly projected onto phenomena by our self-grasping mind. All phenomena naturally appear to our minds to be inherently existent and, without realizing that this appearance is mistaken, we instinctively assent to it and hold phenomena to exist inherently or truly. This is the fundamental reason why we are in samsara.

There are two stages to realizing emptiness. The first stage is clearly to identify the way phenomena appear to our mind to be inherently existent, and how we firmly believe in the truth of this appearance. This is called 'identifying the object of negation'. If our meditation on emptiness is to be effective it is essential that we begin with a very clear image of what is to be negated. The second stage is to refute the object of negation, that is, to prove to ourselves, using various lines of reasoning, that the object of negation does not actually exist. Finally we meditate on the absence of the object of negation.

Because we grasp most strongly at ourselves and our bodies, it is best if we begin by meditating on the emptiness of these two phenomena. Therefore, in the instructions that follow, two meditations are explained: meditation on the emptiness of the I, and meditation on the emptiness of the body.

PREPARATION

We go for refuge, generate a special bodhichitta motivation and complete the other preparatory practices.

Kyabje Trijang Rinpoche

FIRST CONTEMPLATION

The emptiness of the I

Identifying the object of negation

Although we grasp at an inherently existent I all the time, even during sleep, it is not easy to identify how it appears to our mind. Therefore, to begin with, in order to identify it clearly, we must allow it to manifest strongly by contemplating situations in which we have an exaggerated sense of I, such as when we are embarrassed, ashamed, afraid or indignant. We recall, or imagine, such a situation and then, without any comment or analysis, we try to get a clear mental image of how the I naturally appears at such times. We have to be patient at this stage because it may take many sessions before we achieve a clear image. Eventually we shall see that the I appears to be completely solid and real, existing from its own side without depending upon the body or the mind. This vividly appearing I is the inherently existent I that we cherish so strongly. It is the I that we defend when we are criticized, and that we are so proud of when we are praised.

Once we have an image of how the I appears in these extreme circumstances, we try to identify how the I appears normally, in less extreme situations. For example, we can observe the I that is presently meditating and try to discover how it appears to our mind. Eventually we shall see that, although there is not such an inflated sense of I, nevertheless the I still appears to be inherently existent, existing from its own side without depending upon the body or the mind.

Once we have an image of the inherently existent I, we focus on it for a short time with single-pointed concentration, and then we proceed to the second stage.

Refuting the object of negation

If the I exists in the way that it appears, it must exist in one of four ways: as the body, as the mind, as the collection of body and mind, or as something separate from the body and mind. There is no other possibility. We contemplate this carefully until we become convinced that this is the case. Then we proceed to examine each of the four possibilities:

1 If the I is the body, there is no sense in saying 'my body', because the possessor and the possessed are identical.

If the I is the body, there is no rebirth because the I ceases when the body dies.

If the I and the body are identical, then since we are capable of developing faith, dreaming, solving mathematical puzzles, and so on, it follows that flesh, blood and bones can do the same.

Since none of this is true, it follows that the I is not the body.

2 If the I is the mind, there is no sense in saying 'my mind', because the possessor and the possessed are identical. But usually when we focus on our mind we say 'my mind'. This clearly indicates that the I is not the mind.

If the I is the mind, then since each person has many types of mind, such as six consciousnesses, conceptual minds and non-conceptual minds, and so forth, it follows that each person has just as many I's.

Since this is absurd, it follows that the I is not the mind.

3 Since the body is not the I and the mind is not the I, the collection of the body and the mind cannot be the I. The collection of body and mind is a collection of things that are not the I, so how can the collection itself be the I? For example, in a herd of cows none of the animals is a sheep, therefore the herd itself is not sheep. In the same way, in the collection of body and mind, neither the body nor the mind is the I, therefore the collection itself is not the I.

You may find this point difficult to understand, but if you think about it for a long time, with a calm and positive mind, and discuss it with more experienced practitioners it will gradually become clear to you. You can also consult authentic books on the subject such as *Heart of Wisdom*.

4 If the I is not the body, not the mind, and not the collection of body and mind, the only possibility that remains is that it is something separate from the body and mind. If this is the case, we must be able to apprehend the I without either the body or the mind appearing, but if we imagine that our body and our mind were completely to disappear there would be nothing remaining that could be called the I. Therefore it follows that the I is not separate from the body and mind.

We should imagine that our body gradually dissolves into thin air. Then our mind dissolves, our thoughts scatter with the wind, our feelings, wishes and awareness melt into nothingness. Is there anything left that is the I? There is nothing. Clearly the I is not something separate from the body and mind.

We have now examined all four possibilities and have failed to find the I. Since we have already decided that there is no fifth possibility, we must conclude that the truly existent I that normally appears so vividly does not exist at all. Where there previously appeared an inherently existent I, there now appears an absence of that I. This absence is emptiness, the lack of an inherently existent I.

FIRST MEDITATION

We contemplate in this way until there appears to our mind a mental image of the absence of an inherently existent I. This image is our object of meditation. We try to become completely familiar with it by concentrating on it single-pointedly.

Because we have grasped at an inherently existent I since beginningless time, and cherished it more dearly than anything else, the experience of failing to find the I in meditation can be quite shocking at first. Some people develop fear, thinking that they have become completely non-existent. Others feel great joy, as if the source of all their problems is vanishing. Both reactions are good signs and indicate correct meditation. After a while, these initial reactions will subside and our mind will settle into a more balanced state. Then we will be able to meditate on emptiness in a calm, controlled manner. By applying the instructions on concentration from the previous meditation, we should allow our mind to become absorbed in space-like emptiness. It is important to remember that our object is emptiness, the absence of an inherently existent I, not just mere nothingness. Occasionally we should check our meditation with discriminating alertness. If our mind has wandered to another object, or if we have lost the meaning of emptiness and are just focusing on nothingness, we should return to the contemplations in order to bring emptiness clearly to mind once again.

We may wonder, 'If there is no truly existent I, then who is meditating? Who will get up from meditation, speak to others, and reply when my name is called?' Though there is nothing within the body and mind, or separate from the body and mind, that is the I, this does not mean that the I does not exist at all. Although the I does not exist in any of the four ways mentioned above, it does exist conventionally. The I is merely a designation imputed by the conceptual mind on the collection of body and mind. So long as we are satisfied with the mere designation 'I', there is no problem. We can think: 'I exist', 'I am going to town', and so on. The problem arises when we look for an I other than the mere conceptual imputation 'I'. The self-grasping mind holds to an I that ultimately exists, independent of conceptual imputation, as if there were a 'real' I existing behind the label. If such an I existed we would be able to find it, but we have seen that the I cannot be found upon investigation. The conclusion of our search was a definite non-finding of the I. This unfindability of the I is the emptiness of the I, the ultimate nature of the I. The I that exists as mere imputation is the conventional nature of the I.

The emptiness of the body

Identifying the object of negation

The way to meditate on the emptiness of the body is similar to the way to meditate on the emptiness of the I. First the object of negation must be identified.

Normally when we think 'my body', a body that exists from its own side and is a single entity not depending on its parts, appears to our mind. Such a body is the object of negation and is in fact non-existent. 'Truly existent body', 'inherently existent body' and 'body that exists from its own side' all have the same meaning.

Refuting the object of negation

If the body exists as it appears, it must exist in one of two ways: as its parts, or separate from its parts; there is no third possibility.

If the body is one with its parts, is it the individual parts or the collection of its parts? If it is the individual parts, then is it the hands, the face, the skin, the bones, the flesh or the internal organs? By checking carefully 'Is the head the body? Is the flesh the body?' and so on, we will easily see that none of the individual parts of the body is the body.

If the body is not its individual parts, is it the collection of its parts? The collection of the parts of the body cannot be the body. Why? The parts of the body are all non-bodies, so how can a collection of non-bodies be a body? The hands, feet, and so forth are all parts of the body, not the body itself. Even though all these parts are assembled together, this collection remains simply parts; it does not magically transform into the part-possessor, the body.

We should recall how our body appears to us when it is praised or insulted. It appears to be, from its own side, a distinct unit. It does not appear as something that is merely designated as a unit, but which in fact is made up of many separate parts, like a forest, or a herd of cows. Although the body appears as a single entity that exists from its own side without depending upon the limbs, trunk and head, in reality it is merely designated to the collection of those parts. The collection of the parts of the body is an aggregation of many distinct elements that function together. This aggregation may be thought of as a unit, but that unit has no existence independent of its constituent parts.

If the body is not its parts, the only other possibility is that it is separate from its parts; but if all the parts of the body were to disappear there would be nothing left that could be called the body. We should imagine that all the parts of our body melt into light and disappear. First the skin dissolves, then the flesh, blood and internal organs, and finally the skeleton melts and vanishes into light. Is there anything left that is our body? There is nothing. There is no body separate from its parts.

We have now exhausted all possibilities. The body is not its parts and it is not separate from its parts. Clearly, the body cannot be found. Where previously there appeared an inherently existent body, there now appears an absence of that body. This absence is the emptiness of the body, the lack of an inherently existent body.

SECOND MEDITATION

Recognizing this absence to be the lack of an inherently existent body, we meditate on it single-pointedly. Once again, we should examine our meditation with discriminating alertness to make sure that we are meditating on the emptiness of the body and not on nothingness. If we lose the meaning of emptiness, we should return to the contemplations to restore it.

As with the I, the fact that the body cannot be found upon investigation does not imply that the body does not exist at all. The body does exist, but only as a conventional imputation. In accordance with accepted convention, we can impute 'body' to the assembly of limbs, trunk and head; but if we try to pinpoint the body, hoping to find a substantially existent phenomenon to which the word 'body' refers, we find no body. This unfindability of the body is the emptiness of the body, the ultimate nature of the body. The body that exists as mere imputation is the conventional nature of the body.

Although it is incorrect to assert that the body is identical with the collection of the limbs, trunk and head, there is no fault in saying that the body is imputed upon this collection. We should consider that although the parts of the body are plural, the body is singular. 'Body' is simply an imputation made by the mind that imputes it. It does not exist from the object's side. There is no fault in imputing a singular phenomenon to a group of many things. For example, we can impute the singular 'forest' to a group of many trees, or 'herd' to a group of many cows.

All phenomena exist by way of convention; nothing is inherently existent. This applies to mind, Buddha, and even to emptiness itself; everything is merely imputed by mind. All phenomena have parts. Physical phenomena have physical parts and non-physical phenomena have various attributes which can be distinguished by thought. Using the same type of reasoning as above, we can realize that any phenomenon is not one of its parts, not the collection of its parts, and not separate from its parts. In this way we can realize the emptiness of all phenomena. It is particularly helpful to meditate on the emptiness of objects that arouse in us strong delusions such as attachment or anger. By analysing correctly, we will realize that the object we desire, or the object we dislike, does not exist from its own side; its beauty or ugliness, and even its very existence, are imputed by the mind. By thinking in this way we will discover that there is no basis for attachment or hatred.

DEDICATION

We dedicate all the virtues we have created in this meditation practice to the welfare of all living beings by reciting the dedication prayers.

SUBSEQUENT PRACTICE

During the meditation break we should try to recognize that whatever appears to our mind lacks true existence. In a dream things appear vividly to the dreamer, but when the dreamer awakes he or she immediately realizes that the objects that appeared in the dream were just mental appearances that did not exist from their own side. We should view all phenomena in a similar way; though they appear vividly to our mind, they lack inherent existence.

Conclusion

Having developed a good heart towards all living beings, we should engage in the Bodhisattva's way of life by keeping the Bodhisattva vows and practising the six perfections.[30] In particular, we should train in the union of tranquil abiding and superior seeing observing emptiness. By practising in this way we will gradually progress from being an ordinary person to becoming a Bodhisattva. Finally we will become a fully enlightened being, a Buddha.

Appendix 1

THE COMMITMENTS OF GOING FOR REFUGE

When we go for refuge we undertake to observe twelve special commitments. By observing these sincerely we will protect our mind of refuge, and it will gradually become more powerful. These commitments lay the foundation for all the realizations of the Stages of the Path. Realizing this, we should not regard them as a burden, but practise them joyfully and sincerely.

Within the twelve commitments there are six specific commitments and six general commitments. The six specific commitments are so called because they are related specifically to each of the Three Jewels. There are two commitments related to Buddha, two related to Dharma and two related to Sangha. In each case, there is one thing to abandon and one thing to practise. The remaining six commitments apply equally to Buddha, Dharma and Sangha.

These twelve commitments will now be briefly explained.

The two commitments specifically related to Buddha

1 Not to go for refuge in teachers who contradict Buddha's view, or in samsaric gods. By going for refuge in Buddha we have a commitment to abandon going for ultimate refuge in teachers who contradict Buddha's view, or to worldly gods. This does not mean that we cannot receive help from others; it means that we do not rely on others to provide ultimate protection from suffering.

2 To regard any image of Buddha as an actual Buddha. By going for refuge in Buddha we also have a commitment to regard any image of Buddha as an actual Buddha. Whenever we see a statue of Buddha, whether it is made of gold or anything else, we should see it as an actual Buddha. We should disregard the material or the quality of the craftsmanship, and pay homage by making offerings and prostrations, and going for refuge. If we practise like this our merit will increase abundantly.

The two commitments specifically related to Dharma

3 Not to harm others. By going for refuge to Dharma we have a commitment to abandon harming others. Instead of treating others badly, we should try, with the best motivation, to benefit them whenever we can. We first need to concentrate on reducing harmful thoughts and generating a beneficial intention towards those who are close to us, such as our friends and family. When we have developed a good heart towards these people we can gradually extend our practice to include more and more people, until finally we have a good heart towards all living beings. If we can abandon harmful thoughts and always have a beneficial intention, we will easily attain the realizations of great love and great compassion. In this way, from the very beginning of our practice of going for refuge we begin to increase our compassion, which is the very essence of the Buddhadharma.

4 To regard all Dharma scriptures as the actual Dharma Jewel. By going for refuge in Dharma we also have a commitment to regard all Dharma scriptures as the actual Dharma Jewel. Dharma is the source of all health and happiness. Since we cannot see actual Dharma Jewels with our eyes, we need to regard Dharma texts as actual Dharma Jewels, because actual Dharma Jewels arise only as a result of learning, contemplating and meditating on the meaning of the scriptures. We need to respect every letter of the scriptures, and every letter of explanation of Buddha's teaching. Therefore, we must treat Dharma books with great care and avoid walking over them or putting them in inappropriate places where they might be damaged or abused. Each time we neglect or spoil our Dharma books we create the cause to become more ignorant, because these actions are similar to the action of abandoning Dharma. Once the great Tibetan teacher Geshe Sharawa saw some people playing carelessly with their Dharma books and said to them, 'You should not do that. You already have enough ignorance. Why do you want to make yourselves even more ignorant?'

The two commitments specifically related to Sangha

5 Not to allow ourselves to be influenced by people who reject Buddha's teaching. By going for refuge in the Sangha we have a commitment to stop being influenced by people who reject Buddha's teaching. This does not mean that we should abandon these people, merely that we should not let their views influence our mind. Without abandoning love and consideration for others, we need to be vigilant and make sure that we are not being led astray by their bad habits and unsound advice.

6 To regard anyone who wears the robes of an ordained person as an actual Sangha Jewel. By going for refuge in the Sangha we also have a commitment to acknowledge anyone who wears the robes of an ordained person as an actual Sangha Jewel.[29] Even if ordained Sangha are poor, we still need to pay respect to them because they are keeping moral discipline, and this is something very rare and precious.

The six general commitments

7 To go for refuge to the Three Jewels again and again, remembering their good qualities and the differences between them. Dharma is like a boat which can carry us across the ocean of samsara, Buddha is like the skilful navigator of the boat, and the Sangha are like the crew. Remembering this, we should go for refuge again and again to the Three Jewels.

8 To offer the first portion of whatever we eat or drink to the Three Jewels, while remembering their kindness. Since we need to eat and drink several times each day, if we always offer the first portion of our food or drink to the Three Jewels, remembering their kindness, we will greatly increase our merit. We can do this with the following prayer:

> I make this offering to you, Buddha Shakyamuni,
> Whose mind is the synthesis of all Buddha Jewels,
> Whose speech is the synthesis of all Dharma Jewels,
> Whose body is the synthesis of all Sangha Jewels.
> O Blessed One, please accept this and bless my mind.

OM AH HUM   (3x)

It is important always to remember Buddha's kindness. All our happiness is a result of Buddha's kindness. All Buddha's actions are pervaded by compassion and concern for others, and it is these actions that enable us to perform virtuous actions which are the cause of our happiness.

Without Buddha's kindness we would not know the real causes of happiness, or the real causes of suffering. Buddha taught us how all happiness and suffering depend on the mind. He showed us how to abandon those states of mind that cause suffering and cultivate those states of mind that cause happiness. In other words, he taught us perfect methods for overcoming suffering and attaining happiness. No one else us taught these methods. How kind Buddha is!

Our own human body is proof of Buddha's kindness. It is by virtue of Buddha's blessings and instructions that we were able to create the cause to take rebirth in a human form, with all the freedoms and endowments necessary for spiritual practice. If we are now able to learn the Dharma and meet Spiritual Guides, it is only through Buddha's kindness. We can now apply the methods that lead to full enlightenment and gain realizations only because Buddha was kind enough to turn the Wheel of Dharma and show his example in this world. Even the small wisdom we possess to discriminate between what is beneficial and what is harmful, and to identify Buddha's teaching as worthwhile, is a result of Buddha's kindness.

We should not think that Buddha helps only those who follow him. Buddha attained enlightenment in order to benefit all living beings. He manifests in many different forms, sometimes even as non-Buddhist teachers, in order to help others. There is no sentient being who has not benefited from the kindness of Buddha.

9 With compassion, always to encourage others to go for refuge. We should always try to help others go for refuge. However, it is important to be skilful. If we know someone who is interested in Dharma, we should help them to develop the causes of going for refuge: fear of suffering, and faith in the Three Jewels. We can talk to them about impermanence – how the conditions of this life change and how our body will grow old and decay – and we can talk about the sufferings of old age, sickness and death. We can talk about what will happen after death, about the different types of rebirth, and about how all types of rebirth are in the nature of suffering. If we skilfully introduce these thoughts into our conversations, the other person will begin to lose his complacency and, when he starts to feel uncomfortable, he will naturally want to find out what can be done. At this point we can explain about Buddha, Dharma and Sangha, and how they can help us. Then we can explain how to go for refuge.

If we help someone else tactfully in this way, without being arrogant or impatient, we will bring them real benefit. It is never certain that the material gifts we give to others will actually help them; sometimes they even cause more problems. The best way to help others is to lead them into Dharma. If we cannot give elaborate explanations, we can at least give proper advice to those who are unhappy and help them to solve their problems by means of Dharma.

10 To go for refuge at least three times during the day and three times during the night, remembering the benefits of going for refuge.   So that we never forget the Three Jewels we should go for refuge once every four hours, or at least three times during the day and three times during the night. If we never forget the Three Jewels and regularly contemplate the benefits of going for refuge, we will gain realizations very quickly. We should be like a businessman who never forgets his projects even while he is relaxing.

11 To perform every action with complete trust in the Three Jewels.   We should rely on the Three Jewels in everything that we do. In this way all our actions will be successful. There is no need to seek the inspiration and blessings of worldly gods but, by making offerings and requests, we should always try to receive the blessings of Buddha, Dharma and Sangha.

12 Never to forsake the Three Jewels, even at the cost of our life, or even as a joke.   We should never abandon the Three Jewels because going for refuge is the foundation of all Dharma realizations. Once a Buddhist was taken captive and his enemy said to him, 'Give up your refuge in Buddha or I shall kill you.' He refused to forsake his refuge and was killed, but when clairvoyants looked they saw that he had been immediately reborn as a god.

Appendix 2

A SUGGESTED RETREAT SCHEDULE

When we do retreat on the twenty-one meditations it is best if our retreat is at least one week long. If possible we should do four sessions each day. The first session should be early in the morning, the second before lunch, the third in the late afternoon, and the fourth in the evening. We can make the sessions as long as we wish, from half an hour up to two hours each. We should begin each session with the preparatory practices and then engage in the contemplations and meditations according to the sequence suggested below. At the end of each session we should dedicate our merit for the welfare of all living beings, and in between sessions we should try to engage in the subsequent practices with strong mindfulness. If the retreat is longer than one week, we can repeat the cycle each week. In this way, each week we will cover all twenty-one meditations, from relying on a Spiritual Guide to superior seeing.

DAY ONE

Session 1 Meditation 1 – Relying on a Spiritual Guide
Session 2 Meditation 2 – Our precious human life
Session 3 Meditation 3 – Death and impermanence
Session 4 Meditations 4, 5 & 6 – The danger of lower rebirth, refuge practice, and actions and their effects

DAY TWO

Session 1	Meditation 7 – Developing renunciation, using the first four contemplations: birth, ageing, sickness and death
Session 2	Meditation 7 – Developing renunciation, using the remaining three contemplations
Session 3	Meditation 7 – Developing renunciation, using all seven contemplations
Session 4	Meditation 7 – Developing renunciation, using all seven contemplations

DAY THREE

Session 1	Meditation 8 – Developing equanimity
Session 2	Meditation 9 – Recognizing that all sentient beings are our mothers
Session 3	Meditation 10 – Remembering the kindness of sentient beings
Session 4	Meditation 11 – Equalizing self and others

DAY FOUR

Session 1	Meditation 12 – The disadvantages of self-cherishing
Session 2	Meditation 13 – The advantages of cherishing others
Session 3	Meditation 14 – Exchanging self with others
Session 4	Meditation 15 – Great compassion

DAY FIVE

Session 1	Meditation 16 – Taking
Session 2	Meditation 17 – Wishing love
Session 3	Meditation 18 – Giving
Session 4	Meditation 19 – Bodhichitta

DAY SIX

All four   Meditation 20 – Tranquil abiding, using either
sessions   our chosen object or bodhichitta as our
meditation object

DAY SEVEN

All four   Meditation 21 – Superior seeing, meditation
sessions   on emptiness

Notes

1 Hinayana literally means 'Lesser Vehicle'. The aim of a Hinayana practitioner is to achieve his or her own liberation from samsara. Mahayana literally means 'Greater Vehicle'. The aim of a Mahayana practitioner is to achieve Buddhahood in order to benefit all living beings.

2 Dharma is the teachings, practices and spiritual realizations that protect living beings from suffering.

3 A Buddha is a being who has completely purified his or her mind and has brought to perfection all good qualities. A Buddha is not only free from the delusions that bind a person to samsara, but he has also eliminated the unclarity of mind that prevents the direct knowledge of all phenomena.

4 A Bodhisattva is a person with spontaneous bodhichitta.

5 A Spiritual Guide (Guru in Sanskrit, Lama in Tibetan) is a qualified Dharma teacher.

6 Emptiness is the absence of inherent existence, the ultimate nature of phenomena. See Meditation 21.

7 Bodhichitta is the wish to attain Buddhahood for the benefit of all sentient beings.

8 The very subtle mind manifests in ordinary beings only during deep sleep and at the time of death. Advanced Tantric meditators can use the very subtle mind to meditate on emptiness, and in this way they are able swiftly to remove the obstructions to omniscience and become a Buddha. A more detailed explanation can be found in *Clear Light of Bliss*.

9 An energy wind, or prana in Sanskrit, is the mounting wind of a mind. Every mind is associated with its own mounting wind. The function of a mind is to cognize its

object, while the function of its mounting wind is to move the mind to the object. If the mounting wind is impure, the mind is impure, and if the wind is pure, the mind is pure.

10 Karma means action. Every physical, verbal or mental action we perform leaves an imprint, or karmic seed, on our mental continuum. These seeds eventually ripen as pleasant, unpleasant, or neutral experiences, either later in this life or in a future life.

11 Self-grasping is a wrong consciousness that holds phenomena to be inherently existent.

12 A sentient being is anyone who is not yet a Buddha.

13 Mindfulness is a mental factor that keeps our mind continuously on a wholesome object. Alertness acts like a spy, keeping watch over our state of mind, and conscientiousness guards our mind from delusions.

14 A Dharma realization is a firm experience of any aspect of Dharma.

15 The full vajra posture is the perfect cross-legged posture. Buddha Shakyamuni is depicted in this position on the front cover of this book.

16 A Pure Land is a pure world in which there is no suffering. There are many Pure Lands, such as Sukhavati (Blissful Land), the Pure Land of Buddha Amitabha, and Keagra (Dakini Land), the Pure Land of Buddha Vajrayogini.

17 Liberation is complete freedom from samsara. Enlightenment is the state of Buddhahood.

18 Buddhadharma is the teachings of Buddha or a realization of their meaning.

19 A wish-fulfilling jewel is a legendary jewel similar to Aladdin's lamp.

20 The ten non-virtuous actions are: killing, stealing, sexual misconduct, lying, divisive speech, hurtful speech, idle gossip, covetousness, malice, and holding wrong view. See *Joyful Path of Good Fortune*.

21 A valid cognizer is a non-deceptive mind that realizes its

object. There are two types: inferential cognizers and direct cognizers.

22 Geshe Langri Tangpa was a Kadampa Geshe (AD 1054–1123) who was famous for his realization of exchanging self with others. See *Joyful Path of Good Fortune*.

23 Suffering of change is worldly pleasure. It is so called because continued indulgence in it produces discontent.

24 To give fearlessness is to protect others from fear, danger, anxiety, and so forth.

25 The sevenfold cause and effect is a method to generate bodhichitta in which affectionate love is developed primarily by recognizing all sentient beings as our mothers and remembering their kindness.

26 Equalizing and exchanging self with others is a method to develop bodhichitta in which affectionate love is generated principally by means of equalizing self with others, and great compassion by exchanging self with others.

27 A primary mind is a mind that cognizes the general aspect of its object.

28 After we have achieved the ninth mental abiding, we achieve a special bliss of suppleness. This marks the attainment of tranquil abiding. If we continue to meditate, alternating between placement meditation and analysis in order to gain a deeper experience of the object, eventually we will achieve a bliss of suppleness arisen from analysis, which is superior to that arisen from concentration alone. This marks the attainment of superior seeing. After this point, analysis no longer disturbs the stability of our concentration.

29 A Sangha Jewel is any person who has directly realized emptiness.

30 The Bodhisattva Vows and the six perfections are explained in *The Bodhisattva Vows*.

Other books by Geshe Kelsang Gyatso

The Bodhisattva Vows. An explanation of the Bodhisattva vows and the Six Perfections. (Tharpa, 1990.)

Buddhism in the Tibetan Tradition: A Guide. An introduction to Tibetan Buddhism. (Routledge & Kegan Paul, 1984.)

Clear Light of Bliss. An explanation of tantric mahamudra in Vajrayana Buddhism. (2nd edn. Tharpa, 1990.)

Guide to Dakini Land. A commentary to the Highest Yoga Tantra Practice of Vajrayogini. (Tharpa, 1990.)

Heart of Wisdom. A commentary to the *Heart Sutra*. (2nd edn. Tharpa, 1989.)

Joyful Path of Good Fortune. An explanation of the Stages of the Path to Enlightenment. (Tharpa, 1990.)

Meaningful to Behold. A commentary to Shantideva's *Guide to the Bodhisattva's Way of Life*. (3rd edn. Tharpa, 1989.)

Ocean of Nectar. A commentary to Chandrakirti's *Guide to the Middle Way*. (Tharpa, 1990.)

Universal Compassion. A commentary to Bodhisattva Chekhawa's *Training the Mind in Seven Points*. (Tharpa, 1988.)

Also by Geshe Kelsang Gyatso

JOYFUL PATH
OF GOOD FORTUNE
The Stages of the Path to Enlightenment

The *Stages of the Path* (Tib. *lamrim*) is the essence of all the teachings of the Buddha. The original presentation was composed in the eleventh century by the great Indian Buddhist master Atisha who, in a form that is easy to understand and put into practice, skilfully unified all the Buddha's teachings into a complete and integrated sequence designed to lead the practitioner to full enlightenment.

Joyful Path of Good Fortune is one of the clearest and most extensive *lamrim* commentaries available in English. In accordance with the pure unbroken oral tradition passed down from Atisha to contemporary masters such as Geshe Kelsang Gyatso, it preserves the complete authenticity of the original teachings while being ideally suited to modern-day practitioners, revealing practical methods for transforming the mind and gaining peace and happiness for oneself and others.

Included is detailed advice on how to prepare the mind for meditation and a guide for the practitioner through each successive meditative stage, showing its purpose and demonstrating how each brings about a new level of mental development. In this way Geshe Kelsang provides a structured and practical presentation of the entire path to enlightenment, enabling the reader fully to appreciate the essential meaning of Buddha's teachings and apply them in his or her own daily life.

640pp., Outline of the Text, Glossary, Index, £9.95

Tharpa Publications

Tharpa Publications is a publisher of Buddhist books and iconography. Our main purpose is to preserve and make available the full range of Mahayana Buddhist thought and practice by presenting all the stages of the path to full enlightenment. To further this aim we publish original commentaries to major texts as well as other works relevant to the growth and understanding of Buddhism in the West. In this way we hope to provide a comprehensive range of publications for all levels of interest.

If you would like to receive a copy of our catalogue giving details of our books, prints, posters and cards, as well as future publications, please write to:

Tharpa Publications
15 Bendemeer Road
London SW15 1JX
England